The
Grateful Heart

Also by Wilkie Au
Published by Paulist Press

BY WAY OF THE HEART • Winner of the College Theology Society Book Award for 1990

URGINGS OF THE HEART (with Noreen Cannon)

THE ENDURING HEART • Winner of a Catholic Press Association of the United States and Canada Award in 2000

THE DISCERNING HEART (with Noreen Cannon Au) • Winner of a Catholic Press Association of the United States and Canada Award in 2007

The
Grateful Heart

Living the Christian Message

WILKIE AU
and
NOREEN CANNON AU

Paulist Press
New York/Mahwah, NJ

Cover design by Joy Taylor

Book design by Lynn Else

Library of Congress Cataloging-in-Publication Data

Au, Wilkie, 1944–
    The grateful heart : living the Christian message / Wilkie Au and Noreen Cannon Au.
        p. cm.
    Includes bibliographical references and index.
    ISBN 978-0-8091-4735-9 (alk. paper)
1. Gratitude—Religious aspects—Christianity. I. Au, Noreen Cannon, 1945–
II. Title. III. Title: Living the Christian message.
    BV4647.G8A9 2011
    241´.4—dc22

                                                              2010035327

Published by Paulist Press
997 Macarthur Boulevard
Mahwah, New Jersey, 07430

www.paulistpress.com

Printed and bound in the
United States of America

Contents

In memory of William C. Spohn, theologian
and treasured friend, who taught us
by example how to live and how to die
with grateful love.

Acknowledgments

❧

SOMETIMES SIGNIFICANT BLESSINGS go unnamed because they have been so smoothly folded into our everyday life. We realized this, when we began to think about the people we want to thank for helping make this book a reality. Having almost missed the obvious, we quickly got in touch with the gratitude we feel for the chance to once again work together on a meaningful project. When we left religious life about fifteen years ago, we each wondered what outlets for service would open up for us as lay Christians. Now with this our third coauthored book, we are deeply grateful for both the gift of a shared life as a married couple and the gift of a collaborative ministry.

The list of people who have helped us in our writing of this book is too long to include each by name. We want, however, to single out a few individuals, who have supported and inspired us. First, we are grateful to our friend Bill Spohn, who shared so intimately with us his own experience of dying. His e-mail updates in his last year of life remain an inspiration to us and a lasting testimony to how to live and die with grateful love.

Second, we are especially grateful to Deb Pavelek, our research assistant and friend. Thanks to Deb's dedicated work, we were able to benefit from the extensive psychological literature on the various aspects of gratitude that we include in this volume. We also thank Marjorie Devany, a former student, for her poem on finding God in all things, which appears in chapter 7. Finally, we thank Herb Kaighan for allowing us to adapt his meditation on healing and forgiveness, which appears as a spiritual exercise at the end of chapter five.

Portions of some chapters have appeared in somewhat different form in *Presence: An International Journal of Spiritual Direction, Studies in the Spirituality of Jesuits,* and *The Way,* which is a journal of contemporary spirituality that is published by the British Jesuits. We thank the editors for their permission to include those materials here.

W. W. A.
Loyola Marymount University
Los Angeles, California

N. C. A.
C. G. Jung Institute
Los Angeles, California

Gratitude as a Spiritual Path

If the only prayer you say is thank you, that would be
enough.

—MEISTER ECKHART

OUT OF THE wreckage caused by the global economic crisis of
recent years and the financial ruin of those scammed by Wall Street
crooks comes the inspiring story of Kim Rosen who lost her life
savings in the Bernard Madoff Ponzi scheme, but in the process
rediscovered something precious about life. In her book, *Saved by
a Poem*, she shares how her devastating lost led surprisingly to a new
level of gratitude that gave birth to a deeper appreciation for life's
simple pleasures. "I discovered a quality of gratitude for life itself:
this moment of conversation, this breath, this ray of sun on my
back," Rosen states. "When I lost my life's savings, I found myself
opened to life's simple wonders in a way I had never experienced
before. It's not conditional, not based on having something—
money, or security, or health—as opposed to not having it."[1]

In sharing this story of one woman's journey to gratitude,
we introduce the theme of this book and our personal conviction that—whatever our life circumstances and whatever joys
and sorrows make up our individual life story—we can learn to
live in such a way that gratitude becomes the lens through which

we perceive all of life. We do not have to suffer the loss of anything to get in touch with gratitude. And even if we do lose something that we thought we could not live without, we, like Rosen, can still be grateful for what we do have.

FOSTERING A SUSTAINABLE ATTITUDE OF GRATEFULNESS

How can we foster a disposition of gratitude that can be sustained throughout the seasons of our life? This is the question that lies at the heart of this book. The spiritual challenge in this question lies in living with an abiding stance of gratefulness, as opposed to occasionally feeling thankful when something good happens. At first glance, gratitude seems like a simple thing. It is being appreciative for the good things we enjoy and remembering always to say "thank you." We are taught from our earliest age that gratitude contributes to social success as a person and fosters harmonious relationships in society. So for personal and societal reasons, gratitude is generally viewed positively. While popular self-help books and inspirational cards promote the value of gratitude, seldom do they urge us on to reflect more deeply about the importance of gratitude for human and spiritual growth. Rarely are we encouraged to grow to higher and greater levels of gratefulness. When it is regarded as little more than having good manners and thanking people, the spiritual significance of gratitude goes unrecognized!

Living with gratitude is more complicated and challenging than advice columnists and popular "feel-good" books imply. Even though learning to say "thank you" is one of the earliest lessons our parents drum into us, to develop a truly grateful stance is a lifelong challenge. As a spiritual trait, gratitude must undergo a progressive transformation from the external behavior of "good little boys and girls" intent on adult approval to a deeply internalized value of mature adults. The polite habit of always saying "thanks" needs to be developed throughout life so that death finds us to have been molded by profound gratitude. "A kind of valiant gratitude," is the way one spiritual writer describes the attitude of a dying friend. Witnessing the progressive impoverishment of her friend's life, she says, "I have watched her lose the riches of strength, independence, memory, freedom from pain, even, most wrenchingly, her ability to do things for others. As the possessions of body and mind slip away, she holds on with a kind of valiant gratitude to her greatest treasure: her faith in God's loving presence."[2]

In a letter to the Christians at Thessalonica, St. Paul exhorts them to "Rejoice always, pray without ceasing, give thanks in all circumstances" (1 Thess 5:16–18). These parting words may sound fine as a rhetorical finish to a letter of encouragement, but they do not seem realistic enough to be guidelines for Christian living. After all, how is it possible to be happy at all times, to pray without ceasing, and to be grateful for everything we experience in life? Perhaps, we might conclude, Paul's exhortation can serve as an ideal we can strive for, but not something that we can really put into practice. Modern research in psychology, however, suggests that Paul's stringing together the three elements of happiness, prayer, and gratitude contains the secret of living with deep satisfaction and well-being. "Positive psychology," a recently emergent field in psychology, asserts, on one hand, that there is a real connection between gratitude and happiness.[3] On the other hand, a grateful life-stance relies on a kind of awareness born of prayerful attentiveness. So the ancient words of Paul may have more contemporary relevance than first meets the eye!

POSITIVE PSYCHOLOGY AND BEYOND

Positive psychology, in its study of the components of human happiness, can be seen as offshoot of the humanistic or "Third Force" psychology movement founded by Abraham Maslow in the 1960s. Through such works as *The Psychology of Being* and *The Higher Reaches of Human Nature*, Maslow triggered a paradigm shift in personality studies, a change of focus from the study of pathological personalities to what he labeled "self-actualizing" people. He was interested in observing the characteristics of people from all walks of life who excelled as human beings, as well as in their work. In a similar shift from a negative to a positive focus, positive psychology today is redirecting psychology's focus from the traditional concentration on dysfunction to a study of what accounts for happiness (technically termed "subjective well-being") in people. Because they want to establish a credible "science of happiness," positive psychologists are naturally concerned with providing solid empirical verification for their findings. Their willingness to explore vital human concerns, such as personal meaning, freedom, gratitude and love—realities that are not easily subjected to the empirical methods of psychology—represents a favorable development from the perspective of Christian spirituality.

Positive psychologists seek a deeper understanding of gratitude, because they regard it as an ingredient of subjective well-being. Based on the responses of 5,000 participants in a recent study, researchers found that happiness was closely associated with a core set of personal character traits that they labeled "heart strengths": gratitude, hope, zest, and the ability to love and to be loved.[4] Christian spirituality sees the importance of fostering gratitude not only because of its important link to personal well-being, but also because it moves us to a generosity that benefits others. In other words, well-being moves one to self-transcendence and a graciousness that reaches out to others in loving service. Elizabeth Bartlett, a professor of political science in a midwestern university, captures this overflowing gratitude in a journal entry, after her successful heart transplant:

Yet I have found that it is not enough for me to be thankful. I have a desire to do something in return. To do thanks. To give thanks. Give things. Give thoughts. Give love. So gratitude becomes the gift, creating a cycle of giving and receiving, the endless waterfall. Filling up and spilling over. To give from the fullness of my being. This comes not from a feeling of obligation, like a child's obligatory thank-you note to grandmas and aunts and uncles after receiving presents. Rather, it is a spontaneous charitableness, perhaps not even to the giver but to someone else, to whoever crosses one's path. It is the simple passing on of the gift.[5]

Biblical examples also illustrate how gratitude leads spontaneously to the desire to give and serve:

- Zacchaeus, the taxcollector, acknowledges his gratefulness for being seen and given the gift of salvation by pledging: "…half of my possessions, Lord, I will give to the poor; and if I have defrauded anyone of anything, I will pay back four times as much" (Luke 19:8).

- The Gerasene demoniac, once healed by Jesus, volunteers to become a disciple. He goes off to *kerussein*, the technical Greek word in Mark's gospel for preaching the Good News as a chosen disciple. He proceeds to proclaim with gratitude what the Lord had mercifully done for him (Mark 5:19).

- The Samaritan woman at the well becomes an effective preacher of the Word, after her healing encounter with Jesus enabled her to convert the energy she once used to defend an embarrassing lifestyle to an outgoing energy aimed at sharing the Good News of her discovery of the Messiah (John 4:39–42).

GRATITUDE AND DEVELOPMENTAL GROWTH

Grateful living entails growing developmentally. Gratitude has many different levels and exists in various forms. We will discuss the different ways we can experience gratitude and how we can foster gratitude as a virtue that reflects our character. We will also discuss obstacles to gratitude that stem from our personality and family upbringing and from the cultural values that influence us in our daily life. Unlike the Greek philosopher Aristotle, who devalued gratitude, we want to make a case for the tremendous value of gratitude for our psychological well-being and spiritual growth. Aristotle rejected gratitude as a virtue in his ideal of a magnanimous or "great-souled" person. For him, a magnanimous person should be totally self-sufficient and not be demeaned by any hint of inferiority due to being indebted and grateful to others.[6] Aristotle's bias may partially explain why many of us who live in a society that prizes self-reliance so highly do not acknowledge the value of gratitude. Culturally conditioned to be self-made and independent, we resist feeling indebted to others. The Christian view of the mature person, however, is the total opposite of Aristotle's philosophical model. As Christians, we follow the way of Jesus for whom inclusive love, mutuality, and interdependence represent the apex of human development.

THE WAY OF JESUS:
A PATH OF GRATITUDE AND LOVE

The basis of a spirituality of gratitude is the belief that gratitude is a gateway to loving like Jesus. Gratitude serves as a threshold or opening to love, which lies at the heart of the spiritual path taught by Jesus. When confronting the question set forth by a lawyer hoping to trip him up, Jesus summarized "the whole Law, and the Prophets also" by recalling the twofold commandment of love: "You must love the Lord your God with all your heart, with your strength, and with all your mind, and your neighbor as yourself" (Matt 22:34–40; Mark 12:28–34; Luke 10:25–28). Cutting through the morass of pharisaic requirements, Jesus went right to the heart of the matter: love is the sine qua non of Christian life. Neither fulfilling the letter of the law, nor fasting and tithing, but simply loving God with our whole being and others as we love ourselves is the bottom line requirement for living with faithfulness and integrity. This truth, so starkly stated, must have brought a refreshing moment of clarity to those perplexed by the intricacies of the Mosaic Law. With equal force, it can provide a clear focus for us who want to follow a spiritual path today. Jesus' message was uncomplicated: loving is the pathway to God and holiness of life.

LIVING CHRISTIAN FAITH: THE ASCETICAL, THE AESTHETICAL, AND THE GRATEFUL WAY

The challenge for Christians has been to understand more clearly what Christian love entails in practical terms. What, for example, is the proper relationship between loving God and loving the people and things of the earth? How can our love of God and neighbor be sustained and shown in daily life? What attitudes and behaviors help or hinder our living a vital Christian life of love? Reflecting the accumulated wisdom of its past, Christian spirituality offers various "ways" or approaches to growing spiritually. One approach, the ascetical, which is associated with a "redemption-centered" spirituality, highlights the importance of ongoing fidelity and vigilance in living as Christians in the world. Another approach, the aesthetical, which is associated with a "creation-centered" spirituality, focuses on the beauty of the created universe as a gateway to God.

In this book, we present the way of gratefulness as a holistic path that integrates the values of both the ascetical and aesthetical approaches. A holistic approach views things in a complementary (both/and) manner, versus a dichotomous (either/or) manner. Accordingly, the way of gratefulness acknowledges the useful contributions of both the ascetical and the aesthetical traditions, regarding them as distinct, though complementary, approaches to living out the twofold commandment of love. Each approach can contribute in important ways to loving as Christians, even though imbalances and distortions result when an exclusive focus is placed on either. The way of gratitude presented here highlights gratitude as a spiritual path that fosters divine love by cultivating an awareness of the plethora of gifts that flow from God as both Creator and Savior.

THE ASCETICAL WAY:
FOCUSING ON FIDELITY AND VIGILANCE

The word *asceticism* comes from the Greek root *askesis*, the training that athletes go through to prepare for competition. It is applied by Paul to the Christian life, viewed as a race for an imperishable reward (1 Cor 9:24–27). Reflecting this Pauline metaphor for the Christian life, the ascetical way emphasizes self-control, discipline, assertion, and renunciation for the sake of achieving the goal. Another metaphor that grounds an ascetical approach to the Christian life is that of a lifelong spiritual battle in which we struggle between forces of good and evil, light and darkness, grace and sin. Paul graphically describes the nature of this spiritual struggle in his letter to the Romans with words that have an enduring ring because they resonate deeply with the personal experience of people throughout the ages. Like Paul, we, too, live with a divided self. We encounter warring forces within ourselves so strong and autonomous that we often feel helpless and weak. Like Paul, we are perplexed by the mystery of our interior fragmentation. When the apostle declares, "I cannot understand my own behavior," we know what he means. "I do not understand my own actions. For I do not do what I want, but I do the very thing I hate....I can will what is right, but I cannot do it. For I do not do the good I want, but the evil I do not want is what I do....Wretched man that I am! Who will rescue me...?" (Rom 7:15, 18–19, 24). The self-sabotaging self wages war within every man and woman. The ascetical way is meant to support our attempts to love in the midst of weakness and struggles.

Perhaps the most concise gospel illustration of the ascetical way is found in the "way section" in Mark's Gospel (8:22— 10:52). Here Mark uses the word *ho hodos* (meaning "the way") seven times, as he illustrates what is entailed in following Jesus. To be a disciple of Jesus requires that we "take up our cross daily" in imitation of Jesus, whose love was sacrificial because he remained faithful to proclaiming the good news of God's unconditional and merciful love, even at the cost of personal suffering and death. By his example of unswerving fidelity to God's will, Jesus showed how we are called to surrender our lives over to God, trusting in the divine promise to always bring new life from death. Jesus had to repeat his instructions three times, because his disciples were slow to understand and resisted such a radical trust in God. The ascetical way in Christian spirituality acknowledges that our struggles today are identical to those of Jesus' disciples. The process of loving according to the way of Jesus involves a slow and lifelong recognition that our tendency towards selfishness, control, ambition, competition, and our desire to be the first and the greatest can stand in the way of loving like Jesus. Thus, there is the need for ongoing fidelity and vigilance in order to stay faithful to the message of Jesus and to avoid the temptations of "the world, the flesh, and the devil."

The ascetical way focuses on the saving love of God that Jesus revealed through his life and ministry. It embodies the guidelines and practices of Christians throughout the centuries who have attempted to conform their lives to the teachings of Jesus. Positively, the ascetical way supports us in our vulnerability and weakened condition, due to "original sin," and reinforces the values of self-knowledge, discipline, restraint, vigilance, and persistent effort. Today the ascetical way can provide invaluable guidance for us in our efforts to love. It cautions us to guard against a self-centeredness that narcissistically focuses on individual pleasure at the cost of caring for our neighbor. It alerts us to our tendency to place our trust in the false gods of material possessions and power instead of trusting in the living God. In our post-9/11 world, fractured by divisive forces and threatened by an ecological crisis of global proportions, the ascetical way encourages us to love God and neighbor by moderating our desires and preventing greed from damaging others and harming the earth.

Negatively, the ascetical way has been tainted at times by a "no pain, no gain" mentality that exalts suffering as the path to holiness. At its worst, the ascetical tradition placed an unhealthy emphasis on self-mastery and control, based on a suspicion of feelings, the denigration of the body and of sexuality, and a devaluation of earthly values and pleasures. Such distortions so twisted the monastic practices of traditional asceticism, once useful means of purifying the self from egocentric obstacles to loving like Christ, that today many view the word *ascetical* pejoratively. They associate asceticism with an inhumane spirituality, in which degrading humiliation masquerades as humility, life-enhancing and natural impulses are rejected as sinful desire, and submissive acceptance of abuse or deadening self-sacrifice are confused with Christian love. Fortunately, with the enlightenment brought about by Vatican II reforms, such distorted ascetical views have largely been demystified and exposed as dangers to healthy Christian and human growth.

THE AESTHETICAL WAY: FOCUSING ON BEAUTY AND WONDER

According to the Acts of the Apostles, the entrance to the temple was called "the Beautiful Gate" (3:2). This biblical verse is suggestive of the aesthetical approach to spiritual growth, which regards beauty as a gateway to God. It focuses our attention on the burst of God's creative love, which gave birth to the universe more than fifteen billion years ago and continues to sustain it in existence at every moment. Centered on the goodness of creation, the aesthetical way fosters appreciation for the earth as the handiwork of God. "The universe itself is so vast and mysterious that it is more than enough to induce in us that sense of awe and joyful gratitude that played such a role in past religious experience," states a contemporary writer regarding ecological faith. "Rituals of the future will celebrate the wonder of the universe and the mystery of life. They will revolve around the natural processes that have brought life into being, and which continue to sustain it."[7]

A hymn of praise to the God of all creation, Psalm 8 captures the spirit of the aesthetical way. It invites us to wonder at the expanse of the created cosmos—the heavens, the moon, and the stars, all "the work of your fingers" and which you "have established" (v. 3). Even while gazing at the starry night with its beautiful lights, the psalmist marvels at the dignity of the human person whom God has "crowned" with "glory and honor" (v. 5). For this psalmist, the beautiful works of God provide reason for wonder and adoration. The biblical story of Adam and Eve's dwelling in intimacy with God in the garden of creation also reflects the aesthetical approach to the spiritual life.

Emphasizing "original goodness" as opposed to "original sin," this path to spirituality celebrates the marvelous mystery of the human person.

The aesthetical way is based on the fact that "awareness of the divine begins with wonder" because a dominant response to the shock of a wonder-event is the "movement from admiration to contemplation to celebration."[8] By returning us to objects that were given in wonder so that we might prolong admiration and appreciation, contemplation of beauty generates "gratitude and the impulse to celebrate, or possibly even to worship."[9] Reality, when regarded with wonder, alludes to something beyond itself. It is this allusion that conveys to us "the awareness of a spiritual dimension of reality, the relatedness of being to transcendent meaning."[10] Perceiving creation with marvel leads naturally to awe—a sense for the reference everywhere to God who is beyond all created things. The aesthetic way invites us to cultivate this awe-inspired vision of reality that enables us to find God in all things. In short, the aesthetical path reminds us "The world is charged with the grandeur of God" and encourages us to be more attentive to the loving presence of God "like shining from shook foil" throughout the created universe.

A contemporary spiritual writer's account of a prayer experience nicely illustrates how the way of beauty can bring spiritual renewal.

> At one retreat I attended, our leader brought a large book of Georgia O'Keefe's flower paintings. She played a recording of gentle music and invited us to immerse ourselves in receiving beauty. The music and pictures soothed my weary soul. I saw flowers in a new way. I marveled at the depth and beauty at the center of each flower. I let the colors enrich me and smiled at the boldness of O'Keefe's work. I felt renewed and given new sight.[11]

THE GRATEFUL WAY: FOCUSING ON GIFTS AND BLESSINGS

Beauty as a gateway to God can help us to make of the universe a temple, to perceive in the world intimations of the divine, to feel in the rush of the passing the stillness of the eternal, and to sense the ultimate in the simple, common ordinary experiences of our lives. An exclusive focus on the aesthetical way can, however, unwittingly diminish our appreciation of the total scope of God's largess to us. As Jesuit theologian Peter Schineller reminds us,

> While the loving presence of God in creation is a constant, that is not God's full or final word of love. We must proceed, with the witness of the life of Jesus, to see the even greater manifestation of the graceful love of God.[12]

To be true to the Christian path, we cannot lose sight of the self-giving love of Jesus, who incarnated the love of God and whose passion and death was an intensification, a deeper manifestation of the boundless, self-sacrificial love of God. Thus, Schineller rightly states, "The virtue of gratitude is very close to a creation-centered spirituality. But it must be gratitude for the deepest manifestations of the love of God in Jesus Christ who is Creator and Redeemer."[13] Psalm 100 captures this inclusive appreciation of the multiple modes of God's gifts to us in an invitation to praise God:

> Make a joyful noise to the LORD, all the earth.
> > Worship the LORD with gladness;
> > come into his presence with singing.

Know that the LORD is God.
>It is he that made us, and we are his;
>we are his people, and the sheep of his pasture.

Enter his gates with thanksgiving,
>and his courts with praise.
>Give thanks to him, bless his name.

For the LORD is good;
>his steadfast love endures forever,
>and his faithfulness to all generations.

A holistic Christian spirituality recognizes the original blessing that is the gift of creation, as well as all creation's need for healing and redemption. It gratefully acknowledges both the creative and the saving love of God.

In her *Loving Creation*, theologian Kathleen Fischer highlights how St. Francis of Assisi not only exhibited an intimate love for creation—as seen in his gentle encounter with the wolf of Gubbio and his exhortation to the birds to praise their Creator—he also was drawn to live like the poor Christ of the gospel. "Renouncing possessions was a piece with Francis' love of creation," states Fischer, however, "his asceticism never negated the material world nor pronounced it evil."[14] In Francis, we see how the ascetical and aesthetical ways can serve as a pathway to holiness, for he "integrated his gratitude for creation not only with a love for the poor, but also with a commitment to peace and an intense familiarity with the cross of Christ."[15] Clearly, Francis discovered gospel joy through a grateful communion with Brother Sun, Sister Moon, and Mother Earth, not in the pursuit of countless possessions. However, "cosmic empathy of a Franciscan kind," states Jesuit moral theologian Drew Christiansen,

...is not the simple fruit of the contemplation of nature. As healing and satisfying as it may be, nature mysticism does not prepare the heart to care for the outcast leper....Francis' care for leper and wolf alike was prompted by his contemplation of Jesus in the Gospel, a Jesus who sought to be among the little ones, who, emptying Himself of divinity, modeled Himself as a servant to all.[16]

A SPIRITUALITY OF GRATITUDE

This book presents a spirituality of gratitude that reflects the wisdom of both the ascetical and aesthetical approaches. More specifically, it is a spirituality that is rooted in Ignatius Loyola's classic *Spiritual Exercises*, which encourages us to remember "the benefits received, of creation, redemption, and particular gifts, pondering with much feeling how much God...has done for me, and how much [God] has given me of what [God] has, and then the same [God]desires to give me [God's self]...."[17] The *Spiritual Exercises* provides a rich illustration of how gratitude enables us to acknowledge the love of God in all its manifestations—not only in creation, but also in the life, death, and resurrection of Jesus. In chapter two, we elaborate in detail how gratitude constitutes a central motif of the *Spiritual Exercises*. Without doubt, Ignatius saw gratitude as a spiritual pathway to loving God and others.

A spirituality of gratitude must lead us beyond the subjective well-being espoused by positive psychology to a holiness that is at once earthy and mystical. German theologian Dietrich Bonhoeffer talked about the benefit of gratitude when he said, "In ordinary life we hardly realize that we receive a great deal more than we give, and that it is only with gratitude that life becomes rich."[18] And the richness that gratitude brings includes spiritual transformation. The late Indian Jesuit, Anthony de Mello, aptly described the heart of a spirituality of gratitude when he said, "Mysticism is felt-gratitude for everything." Mysticism is neither esoteric nor ethereal. It entails knowing something in a way that pervades our whole being, not just in a purely conceptual, heady way. "To some the truth of God never comes closer than a logical conclusion" a philosopher once remarked, but "to the mystic God becomes real in the same sense that experienced beauty is real, or the feel of spring is real or that summer sunlight is real."[19] Mystical knowing is based on first-hand experience.

> All our senses are given to us to enjoy, and to praise God. The smell of the sea, the blossom borne on the wind, of the soft flesh of a little baby; the taste of ripe plum or bread fresh from the oven, the feel of warm cat's fur, or the body of a lover—these are all forms of thanksgiving prayer.[20]

Grounded in solid sense knowledge that is affective and personal, felt-gratitude for everything is deeply transformative. It shapes us into Christians whose deep sense of the gift-nature of everything turns us towards God and others with thanksgiving and love, and thus can serve as a reliable pathway to God and spiritual fulfillment.

CHAPTER 1

Gratitude as a Life-Giving Practice

❧

All goods look better when they look like gifts.
—G. K. CHESTERTON[1]

GRATITUDE TAKES ON many forms. As an emotion, it refers to the spontaneous surge of feeling for someone who does something good for us. As a virtue, it is something that we have developed through years of practice so that being grateful has become a habitual part of our character. And as an attitude, it is gratefulness for everything in life, including our very existence from moment to moment. In all these manifestations, gratitude has been regarded throughout history as a life-giving practice that benefits both individuals and society. All major religions foster gratitude, because it possesses a spiritual quality and is a distinguishing mark of religious development.

In recent years, the research of positive psychologists has begun to verify common assumptions about the benefits of gratitude, such as producing peace of mind, more satisfying personal relationships, and happiness in general. Implicit in self-help efforts to foster gratitude, for example, is the belief that regular practice of grateful thinking enhances psychological and physical well-being. This belief has been supported by the results of three experiments that investigated the effects of gratitude intervention on psychological and social functioning. The participants in these studies were divided into three groups, each of which was instructed to keep a different type of journal. One group recorded daily events, another recorded hassles, and the third group listed what they were grateful for. The data showed that the people who kept a gratitude journal felt better about their life as a whole and more hopeful about the future than members of either of the other two groups. The gratitude journal increased the participants' experience of gratitude—sparked, for example, by satisfying social encounters, awareness of good health, overcoming hardships, and simply being alive. Participants in the gratitude journal group reported that they felt more joyful, enthusiastic, alert, focused, excited, determined, and stronger, than did those in the group that kept track of their hassles.[2] Other studies have provided helpful insights into the experience of people who possess a grateful disposition versus those who are disinclined to be grateful.[3] Relying on these and other findings of positive psychology, we will highlight how Christian spirituality is an invaluable resource for cultivating gratitude in life. And, more importantly, we will illustrate how gratitude—by making us more compassionate, more likely to help others, less materialistic, and more content with life—can contribute to our growth as Christians.

THE GRATEFUL LEPER SHOWS US THE WAY

Luke's Gospel recounts the story of the grateful leper, the only one of ten lepers cured by Jesus to return to give thanks (17:11–19). Finding himself cured as he made his way home, he "turned back, praising God with a loud voice. He prostrated himself at Jesus' feet and thanked him" (vv. 15–16). His exuberant expression of gratitude is understandable because this fortunate leper was twice blessed. Like the other nine who sought a cure from Jesus, his most obvious blessing was the restoration of physical health. But, unlike the others who did not return to give thanks, this grateful leper received another gift: the precious human capacity to appreciate the goodness of his life. Perhaps, for the first time in his life, this leper was able to look in the mirror with appreciation and say a grateful "yes" to his beauty as a person. He raced back to thank Jesus because he realized that he was healed not only of his leprosy, but also of his self-depreciation and self-rejection. Clearly, the restoration of appreciation gave birth to gratitude.

Jesus holds this grateful leper up as an example to us, when he wonders out loud, "Were not ten made clean? But the other nine, where are they? Was none of them found to return and give praise to God except this foreigner?" (vv. 18–19). Jesus' question about why the other nine lepers did not return to give thanks can elicit many different explanations. A contemporary and novel response to Jesus' question is suggested by the psychological research regarding the disposition toward gratitude, which we describe in the following section.

THE GRATEFUL DISPOSITION

The disposition toward gratitude can be understood as an inclination or proneness to notice the good things that others do for us, along with a prompt readiness to express our feelings of gratitude.[4] As an affective trait, a grateful disposition characterizes some of us more than others. Researchers use four facets of gratitude to distinguish dispositionally grateful people from less dispositionally grateful people.[5] Compared to less grateful individuals, highly grateful people may feel gratitude more *intensely* when something positive happens to them. A second facet of gratitude is *frequency*. Dispositionally grateful people are appreciative of even the simplest favor or act of kindness and tend to report feeling grateful many times daily, while people less disposed toward gratitude experience gratitude less frequently. A third facet is termed *span*. Gratitude span has to do with the number of benefits or life circumstances for which people feel grateful at any given time (e.g., for their families, their friends, their work, their health, and life itself, along with a variety of other blessings). People less disposed to being grateful might experience gratitude for few aspects of their lives. The fourth facet of the disposition toward gratitude is *density*, which refers to the number of people to whom one feels grateful when something positive happens. For example, when asked to whom they are grateful, Olympian gold medalists who are dispositionally grateful people might recite a litany of many people, including their coach, trainer, parents, friends, and God. Those less disposed toward gratitude might feel grateful to fewer people for their achievement.

Luke's grateful leper serves as an illustration of a person who is disposed to being grateful, while the other nine lepers can be seen as less gratefully disposed. The intensity of his gratitude is clear when he rushed back "praising God with a loud voice," and giving thanks to Jesus on bended knees. Perhaps he already thanked Jesus once, at the moment of his cure. But in reflecting more on what just happened to him, it dawned on him what a remarkable gift he had received. No wonder he ran back to express his gratitude again. Jesus not only cured his skin disease, but also restored his precious capacity to appreciate the beauty in life, starting with himself. His gratitude span allowed him to notice the fullness of Jesus' largess. Perhaps, praying in thanksgiving for this life-transforming experience remained a frequent part of his prayer for the rest of his life! And perhaps in later reflection, he felt grateful not only for Jesus, but also for those who told him about Jesus, as well as the other nine lepers who accompanied him in their desperate search for a cure. Of course, Luke does not say any of this, but our conjectures spring from our perception of this grateful leper as fitting the profile of a person with a grateful disposition!

HOW GRATITUDE IS LINKED TO CHRISTIAN LIVING

It is not hard to appreciate the importance of gratitude to Christian growth, when we consider what studies of the grateful disposition have revealed. The research found that people with a grateful disposition, compared to their less grateful counterparts, are generally more peacefully settled in life.[6] On one hand, they "tend to experience positive emotions more often, enjoy greater satisfaction with life and more hope." And on the other hand, they "tend to experience less depression, anxiety, and envy." The study also noted that the more gratefully disposed people "tend to be more empathic, forgiving, helpful, and supportive as well as less focused on materialistic pursuits than are their less grateful counterparts." Placing less importance on material goods, they were less likely to evaluate their own or others' success in terms of possessions and more likely to share their possessions with others. Another study, comparing how feelings of anger, gratitude, guilt, and pride influence our ability to trust, concluded that "anger decreased trust and gratitude increased trust."[7] Certainly, trust, which is the willingness to rely on others, is a pre-requisite of Christian faith and central to Christian discipleship. It is not surprising, then, that the study of the disposition for gratitude found that those prone to be grateful regularly attend religious services and engage in spiritual activities, such as the prayerful reading of religious materials.

These research findings make amply clear that a grateful stance in life increases our capacity to be like Jesus, whose life and message centered on inclusive love, compassionate service, radical trust in God, forgiveness, freedom from anxiety, and dependence on God. Informed by Jesus' example, authentic gratitude for Christians is grounded in poverty of spirit and a deeply felt sense of radical dependence on God. It is also rooted in a peaceful acceptance of personal limitation that welcomes interdependence as part of human life, not something to be ashamed of and shunned. Acknowledging God's and others' gracious generosity, Christian gratitude stems from a profound realization of the gratuity or gift-nature of everything.

PAYING ATTENTION TO OUR DISPOSITION TOWARD GRATITUDE

The four facets of the grateful disposition—intensity, frequency, span, and density—can serve as helpful barometers for us as we commit ourselves to growing in our practice of gratitude. As a spiritual practice, we might periodically consider such questions as:

- How intensely do I experience my moments of gratitude? Can I deepen my experience of gratitude by savoring with more appreciation those people and things that make me feel grateful?

- How often do I stop to consider the blessings and gifts in my life? Would more frequent reflection, perhaps daily, on what make my life full increase my disposition toward gratitude?

- When considering events and people for whom I am grateful, are there gaps in my awareness because I tend to take for granted certain events and people (like family meals and dinner with good friends) because they are so much a part of my ordinary experience?

- When rejoicing over a success or achievement, do I spend enough time to think about all the people who, in some way or other, have contributed to my experience?

EXPANDING OUR GRATITUDE SPAN

Sometimes we get in touch with our blessings only when we are threatened with losing them. Close calls or the prospect of terminal illness rouse us from our complacency and renew our appreciation for the preciousness of life itself. Such gratitude-producing experiences are as common as receiving a negative result on a biopsy, or walking away unharmed from an accident that has totaled our car, or watching as a raging brush fire sweeps down a canyon and mysteriously leapfrogs over our house, sparing us from its voracious flames. It is easy to feel gratitude at moments such as these. To live spiritually vital lives, however, requires that we make gratitude a habitual attitude, not just something we feel when tragedy has been averted.

At age ninety-nine, Marian Olson, a family member, has graciously been helping us with our work on this book. We thought it would be interesting and inspiring to see what her gratitude list would look like. After sending two installments, she wrote, "Although you didn't ask for more, the longer I live the more I find to be grateful for. Every day is a gift, and I'm grateful that I am aware of it." Prefacing her list with "Ninety-nine is good enough for me," she shares, "I'm grateful for:

- An especially good sleep last night
- Being able to remember something different everyday
- The loving attention of my family
- Being able to tie my own shoes

- 20/20 vision (with glasses!)
- My appetite for life
- My wonderful dentist
- Being able to manicure my own fingernails
- Remembering who gave me which gifts
- My taste buds
- Getting to the bathroom on time!

It is typical for many of us to find that we go for days or even weeks at a time without spontaneously turning to God in gratitude. Our activities and concerns can so consume our waking day that when we turn to God at all, it is because we need help. If gratitude is not part of our everyday life, a simple exercise such as the following can heighten our awareness of the blessings we may take for granted:

Lie on the floor or on your bed while you do this exercise.

Imagine you are lying in a hospital bed paralyzed. Imagine that you cannot move a single limb of your body from neck down....

Now with the eyes of your imagination, go through your whole day as a paralyzed person....What do you do all day?...What do you think?...What do you feel?...How do you keep yourself occupied?...

In this paralyzed condition, be aware that you still have your sight. Be grateful for that.

Then become aware that you have your hearing. Be grateful for that too.

Then become aware that you can still think clearly... that you can speak and express yourself...that you have the sense of taste which brings you pleasure.... Be grateful for each of these gifts of God....Realize how rich you are in spite of your paralysis!

Now imagine that your body is beginning to respond well to your physical therapy. It is now possible for you to move your neck and turn your head from side to side, painfully at first, then with greater ease...gradually a much wider range of vision is offered to you. It's possible for you now to look from one end of the ward to the other without having to have your whole body turned by someone....Notice how thankful you feel for this too.

Now return to your present existence and realize that you are not paralyzed. Wriggle your fingers gently and realize there is life and movement in them. Curl and uncurl your toes...flex your arms...bend your legs...Say a prayer of thanksgiving to God over each one of these limbs.[8]

Joy will permeate our days when we can keep alive a sense of gratitude for all God's gifts—both large and small.

FOSTERING AN ATTITUDE OF GRATITUDE

Maintaining an attitude of gratitude requires an ahead-of-time willingness to regard life with appreciation. It involves a conscious choice, an antecedent predisposition, to see the glass as half full rather than half empty. To live with gratitude is to enter reverently into the garden of creation to witness there the presence of God, who at every moment keeps all things in existence.

Julian of Norwich, a fourteenth-century mystic, models a faith that sustains wonder and appreciation for life even in tumultuous times. Hers was a century wracked by pain and chaos: the black plague was devastating Europe, causing disaster on an unprecedented scale (not unlike the global AIDS epidemic); severe crop failures threatened the onslaught of famine at a time when the economic resources of both England and France had been completely drained by the Hundred Years' War; and Europe was convulsing through a complex transition triggered by the demise of feudalism and the emergence of nationalism and the mercantile system (not unlike the upheaval in Russia after the break-up of the Soviet Union and the switch from a centralized to a free-market economy).

Surrounded by these chaotic conditions, Julian was still able to live with trust and gratitude; her religious experience revealed to her that in the end, "all will be well." She was reassured that no matter how fragile life seems, God, like our clothing, "wraps and enfolds us for love, embraces us and shelters us, surrounds us for love...."[9] This wondrous insight came to her as she contemplated an image of something tiny in her hand, not much bigger than a hazelnut. As she gazed at this small object, she was amazed at its ongoing existence. How is something so tiny and fragile able to survive in a universe so fraught with dangers? Her heart was then illuminated to understand that the tiny object before her, as well as everything else in the universe, are held safely together in God's hands.

> It lasts and always will last because God loves it; and thus everything has being through the love of God. In this little thing I saw three properties. The first is that God made it, the second is that God loves it, and the third is that God preserves it.[10]

Julian's insight grounds gratitude in the simple fact that everything is gift. Our response as thankful recipients need simply be one of praise to God, "from whom all blessings flow." Because all we are and all we have are given to us, gratitude is the primary response to life. Gratitude is the only thing we can give. As a life stance, gratitude moves us to cherish everything as a gift to be cared for, nurtured, and brought to fulfillment. The Christian community recognizes the significance of gratitude by making the Eucharist its central act of worship. Literally meaning "thanksgiving," the Eucharist invites us to open our hands and hearts to the Giver of all gifts, and reminds us that life is not to be owned or possessed, but to be shared and finally to be given away. An attitude of gratitude invites us to focus on abundance rather than scarcity, plenty rather than paucity. When we feel that there is more than enough to go around, we are moved to big-heartedness and generous sharing.

THE STRUGGLE TO BE GRATEFUL

Proneness to gratitude varies with individuals. Some of us are more inclined to see "the glass half full" and others of us as "half empty." When we see the glass as totally empty, we tend towards depression; when we sense that the glass is full of bad and painful things, we get resentful. What affects our proneness to certain moods and emotional responses is psychologically complex. At times, it is traceable to genetic predisposition. A Minnesota study of twins, for example, discovered that genetics was responsible for about half of the variability for both positive moods, such as joy and affection, and negative moods such as anxiety and grief. The symbiotic connection between personality characteristics and emotional well-being prompted David Lykken and Auke Tellegen, who conducted the research on twins, to assert that happiness may be a function of "the great genetic lottery that occurs at conception."[11] In other words, some of us are "genetically programmed to be happy most of the time, while others are apparently doomed to go through life per-

petually scowling," asserts Robert Emmons, one of the major figures in current gratitude research.[12]

Genetic predisposition, however, is only half of the story;
the other half has to do with life circumstances and intentional
activities that we engage in to influence our moods. Specifically,
research by positive psychologists has shown that while 50 percent of happiness has to do with genetics, 40 percent has to do
with our intentional activities and 10 percent is circumstantial—
e.g. where we live, our health, our work, our marriage, etc. Such
circumstances of life can be difficult to change, but it is surprising to many that circumstances do not account for as much of
our subjective well-being or happiness as we might think.

Life circumstances do not guarantee sustained happiness,
because we habituate to whatever circumstances we find ourselves in. We get used to such things as the new car, a stellar performance evaluation at work, and the newly remodeled kitchen,
each of which initially made us feel great. An often-cited study of
lottery winners, for example, found that they were no happier
than control groups a year later. Getting out of a depressing
work situation may give a temporary boost to our happiness, but
sustaining that good feeling requires deliberate choices regarding how we act and think.

Researchers theorize that each of us has a characteristic
level of happiness, or happiness set point, to which we inevitably
return following disruptive life events, whether good or bad.
This process of return is called *adaptation*. Initially, changed circumstances elicit a strong reaction in us, but eventually the
strong emotional reaction loses its steam. We adapt in such a way
that, over time, we take good things for granted and accommo-
date to the obstacles we encounter in life, returning once again
to the happiness level that is natural for us. These concepts of set
point and adaptation, however, should not discourage us by
making us think that "trying to become happier may be as futile
as trying to become taller."[13]

Because the biologically programmed set point is not so much a fixed point but a range, it is reasonable to believe that intentional activities—such as the spiritual practices of gratitude that we suggest throughout this book—can influence our happiness. In striving to improve our happiness level, however, we need to be realistic. While the research of positive psychology has shown that how we choose to react to life events can affect our moods, we still do not know "whether our reactions can, in fact, alter the process of adaptation itself and allow us to permanently improve our personal range of happiness."[14]

There are times when our proneness to certain emotional responses is influenced by early childhood experiences. People prone to envy, for example, can often trace the roots of this disposition to their early childhood experience. According to psychoanalyst Melanie Kline, an infant's experience of its mother as either giving or withholding determines whether envy becomes a problem in later life. The psychic roots of our predisposition to gratitude can be similarly complex. Experiences of childhood abandonment, rejection, abuse, and deprivation have long-term effects on our emotional life. Such negative experiences in early childhood can result in a narcissistic personality that is disinclined to be grateful. A painful part of the wound caused by childhood abandonment is a pendulum swing between a deflated sense of worthlessness and a sense of grandiosity. When in the grips of an exaggerated sense of self-importance, the narcissistically wounded have a tendency to believe that they deserve special treatment and privileges without needing to take on reciprocal responsibilities. This sense of entitlement and insensitivity to the needs of others thwart gratitude, because when we feel entitled to everything, we end up thankful for nothing.

In addition to entitlement, researchers point to a number of other attitudes that militate against a grateful outlook on life.[15] These attitudes will be more fully discussed in subsequent chapters, but it would be helpful to summarize them here. They include:

- an inability to admit shortcomings and limitations
- feelings of envy and resentment
- an overemphasis on materialistic values
- the perception of being a victim

Some of these obstacles to being grateful are likely to be deeply ingrained in one's personality and others are constantly reinforced by the materialism of a consumerist society. Understanding our vulnerability to these gratitude-inhibiting attitudes and appreciating the counterbalancing values of Christian spirituality can help us expand our disposition toward gratitude.

MORE TO GRATITUDE THAN MEETS THE EYE

When we analyze the dynamics of various examples of gratitude, we come quickly to realize that it is a more complex reality than first appears. Take, for example, what pastoral theologian Seward Hiltner calls "reactive gratitude." This form of gratitude is seen when initial feelings of thankfulness to someone who has just done us a favor or benefited us through some gift or special consideration are gradually overshadowed by resentment toward them. Upon receiving a favor, our immediate reaction may be one of gratitude, but upon reflection, we realize that "people who have the ability to do something sterling for us have, thereby, a power in relation to us. What happens in reactive gratitude is that, for a time, we forget the power and enjoy the gift." But, once we have gotten used to the gift, "then we begin to react, perhaps unconsciously, against the power that the other held over us, even though he has used it benevolently.

Even with a good and needed gift, the power of the other to give it reminds us of our dependency."[16] In psychoanalytic terms, this feeling of dependency can reactivate an infantile sense of helplessness and accompanying resentment. Reactive gratitude begins with honest feelings of appreciation for a gift and only later does resentment about the power of the giver result in a depreciation of the gift. The transformation of reactive gratitude to a more genuine and sustained gratefulness requires our working through our resentment, which taints the experience of gratitude.

Another inauthentic form of gratitude is what Hiltner calls "pseudo-gratitude." This occurs in situations in which "expressions of thanks, which are sometimes effusive, are actually used to divert attention, of the self or the others, away from where it ought to be."[17] Early in his practice, Freud perceived that this form of gratitude expressed by his patients could divert them from dealing with their real issues and so he began charging a fee to circumvent this pseudo-gratitude from being used as a defensive strategy. When recovering alcoholics, for example, effusively thank their sponsor and others for their help, experienced addiction counselors become concerned lest this become a defensive diversion away from confronting their problem. A more commonplace example of pseudo-gratitude is when we thank a person for being patient when it would be more fitting to apologize for keeping them waiting. An editorial piece in the *British Medical Journal* offers another illustration of what appears to be pseudo-gratitude. The ill-treatment of U.S. military veterans at Walter Reed Army Hospital in Washington, DC, the author suggests, highlights the shielding of Americans from the human cost of war. Based on this, he suggests that the verbal praise and gratitude professed to the troops is "hollow."[18]

Furthermore, "to have the virtue of gratitude is to be disposed...not just to be grateful, but to be grateful in the right way, to the right people, for the right things."[19] Growing in gratitude requires that we reflect concretely on the forms gratitude takes in our life.

Being Grateful in the Right Way: Excessive gratitude can come across as insincere and ingratiating. Repeated and effusive "thank yous" can make us uncomfortable, and even wonder at times what the grateful person really wants. Or a person might say "thank you" only to entice us to give even more. Another false form of gratitude is expressing thanks as a rhetorical ploy to win favor with one's audience or for the sake of making a favorable self-presentation. Then there are times when gratitude is used to flatter and manipulate those in authority and power. If we feel that gratitude is expected of us by people who can affect our lives, our gratitude can be feigned, reflecting our fear rather than our thankfulness.

Being Grateful to the Right People: At awards ceremonies, it is not uncommon to hear honorees express their thanks to those who have contributed to their success. At the Academy Awards ceremony in 1982, for example, Maureen Stapleton told the audience "I would like to thank my family, my children, my friends, and everyone I have ever met in my entire life." No doubt, her exaggerated thanks to everyone she had ever met can be explained by her excitement at the moment. Nevertheless, her statement does point to what researchers refer to as a "shallow gratitude" often heard in public acknowledgments of outside help.[20] Such public acknowledgments are somewhat surprising in light of research findings suggesting that people, in private, tend to claim the credit for themselves and attribute their success to personal strengths! Inside, they somehow feel that acknowledging others' help diminishes their achievement and reduces their own credit. These insincere and shallow-sounding expressions of thanks in public seem to arise from the need to present themselves favorably (i.e., modest and magnanimous), and to avoid blatantly self-serving comments that would draw criticism from others.

On a more profound level, our gratitude is often flawed because we do not sincerely express thanks to God, "in whom we live and breathe, and have our being." In this, we are not unlike our Semitic ancestors. A recurrent theme in the Hebrew Bible is the Israelites' ingratitude to the God of the Covenant who delivered them from the bondage of slavery and led them through the desert into a land flowing with milk and honey. They repeatedly forgot that the God of Abraham, Isaac, and Jacob—not foreign gods—should be the one and only object of their gratitude. Besides forgetting to thank God, there is also the common tendency to forget to be grateful for family members, whose kindness to us is often taken for granted or seen as a right. Parents with ungrateful adolescents who never seem to say "thank you" can perhaps find a ray of hope in Hiltner's insightful reframing of this common family occurrence. "I suspect that adult society has long tried to evoke gratitude from its adolescents," he states, "basically as a means of keeping them under control by acknowledging their power. Adolescent attempts to not feel grateful, therefore, can be stimuli to a new kind of self-responsibility." If Hiltner is correct, there still remains the challenge of moving beyond this development stage of adolescence to a mature ability to express genuine gratitude. In general, it seems clear that when people are told that they "should be thankful," they can feel this imposed or obligatory gratitude as patronizing and demeaning.

Being Grateful for the Right Things: While Christians count a strong disposition to feel grateful as a virtue, this does not mean that all situations equally warrant gratitude. If, for example, people feel deeply grateful for monetary favors (say, stock-market tips) that are not particularly needed (since they have all the money they need), but feel no gratitude to their parents for providing continuing love and support, we would not likely attribute the virtue of gratitude to those persons. Their gratitude seems misguided or trivial and, therefore, not worthy to be considered a virtue that contributes to their real well-being.[21] The same can be said about being grateful for a bribe or favor that compromises our ability to be honest or just. In Luke's Gospel, we see counterfeit gratitude that is actually a cloak for self-righteousness, when we hear the Pharisee's prayer: "God, I thank you that I am not like other people: thieves, rogues, adulterers, or even like this tax collector" (18:11).

GROWING IN GRATEFUL LIVING

Because of the complexities involved in being grateful, it is not spiritually or psychologically helpful to judge ourselves harshly when gratitude is something we struggle with. Understanding the roots of our emotional responses, and seeking change through prayer, therapy, or spiritual direction, can help us expand our capacity for gratitude, and thus add to our personal well-being and spiritual development. Some psychologists observe that gratitude has been seen as both a pleasure and as a virtue. "It is virtuously pleasant because experiencing it not only uplifts the person who experiences it but also edifies the person to whom it is directed," they assert. But the fact that gratitude is considered by people to be a virtue, and not simply a pleasure, "also points to the fact that it does not always come naturally or easily. *Gratitude must, and can, be cultivated.* And by cultivating the virtue, it appears that people may get the pleasure of gratitude, and all of its other attendant benefits, thrown in for free."[22]

Sometimes a simple practice can help expand our gratitude and alter debilitating moods. In describing herself as a recovering pessimist, Karen Reivich, PhD, a research associate at the University of Pennsylvania, states, "Part of my brain is always scanning the horizon for danger." Instead of dismissing her concerns as unwarranted, Reivich created a simple practice to help herself to counter the dour, gloomy part of her personality. "I've created an 'awe wall' covered with poems, my children's photos, a picture of a lavender farm," she shares. "And every day I work on it a bit. I may add a cartoon that made me laugh and a picture drawn by my young son. It's hard to be basking in all these reminders of wonder and simultaneously be filled with dread." According to Reivich and other researchers, strategies like these, employed consistently over time, lead to long-lasting change. She reports that her pessimistic habits are starting to atrophy.

> At first the change happens at the surface, in a conscious change in behavior; then it begins to take place more deeply, becoming almost effortless. That's because I'm repeating the exercise until it becomes a new habit. If I focus my attention on noting good and thinking about the things I can control, I'm using my attention and energy to build optimism and happiness rather than to deepen worry and sadness.[23]

Sometimes, gratitude can be revived by a shift in perspective that enables us to see more clearly the ordinary blessings that we easily overlook, because we are preoccupied by what causes us displeasure. The following story is a humorous illustration of this. A disciple complained:

> "I am in desperate need of help—or I'll go crazy. We're living in a single room—my wife, my children and my in-laws. So our nerves are on edge, we yell and scream at one another. The room is a hell."
> "Do you promise to do whatever I tell you?" said the Master gravely.
> "I swear I shall do anything."

"Very well. How many animals do you have?"

"A cow, a goat and six chickens."

"Take them all into the room with you. Then come back after a week."

The disciple was appalled. But he had promised to obey! So he took the animals in. A week later he came back, a pitiable figure, moaning, "I'm a nervous wreck. The dirt! The stench! The noise! We're all on the verge of madness!"

"Go back," said the Master, "and put the animals out."

The man ran all the way home. And came back the following day, his eyes sparkling with joy. "How sweet life is! The animals are out. The home is a Paradise— so quiet and clean and roomy!"[24]

When we dwell on how life does not unfold according to our expectations, we feel resentful. On the other hand, when we accept that life is a mystery to be entered into, we are able to be grateful for the gift of our lives—even when we cannot make sense of all that happens.

GRATITUDE AS THANKFULNESS AND AS GRATEFULNESS

From a spiritual point of view, Brother David Steindl-Rast, the best-known Catholic proponent of a spirituality of gratitude, asserts the importance of distinguishing between thankfulness and gratefulness, between personal and transpersonal gratitude. "Transpersonal gratitude," he explains, "belongs to our inner realm and we often find no words for it; personal gratitude belongs to the social realm and we most often express it."[25] We express personal gratitude, for example, when we feel thankful for some benefit we have received from someone who gives to us out of a sense of kindness. In contrast, our feeling of gratefulness is a spontaneous response sparked off by being caught up or enthralled by something wonderful, like the starry sky that fills us with spontaneous awe and marvel. It is the thrilling experience of being captivated by a wondrous event or rendered breathless by a beautiful object. At such times, we feel a sense of deep contentment with everything in our existence and grateful to be alive. In short, "Being grateful is a state; thanking is an action."[26]

Gratefulness moves beyond our ordinary experiences of thankfulness in daily life and resembles Abraham Maslow's notion of "peak experiences." Peak experiences are ecstatic moments of spiritual awareness and overwhelming gratefulness. They are often inspired by intense feelings of love, exposure to great music or the breath-taking beauty of nature. Neither planned nor brought about by design, these experiences just happen, as when we are "surprised by joy." "Gratefulness," Steindl-Rast describes with simple elegance, "is an existential 'Wow' before any interpretation."[27]

In his discussions with positive psychologists, Steindl-Rast has argued that the study of gratitude is incomplete, if it does not include gratefulness, which he describes "as the mystical dimension of gratitude." Briefly stated, his point is that "For scientists who explore the religious and spiritual significance of gratitude, it is of prime importance to focus on gratefulness."[28] He grants that conceptualizing gratitude in terms of the three components of thanksgiving—a benefit, a beneficiary, and a benefactor—has facilitated the analytic and experimental study of gratitude. Nevertheless, he argues that the "construal of gratitude in terms of beneficiary, benefice, and benefactor is closely tied up with theistic theology. It produces many valuable insights regarding thankfulness but is ill-equipped to deal with gratefulness."[29]

It is important here to understand Steindl-Rast's allusion to how referring to a theistic notion of God as a person when giving thanks raises some difficulty. People, for example, may experience a profound blessing that they attribute to God's loving care, yet feel uncomfortable with theistic language referring to God as "a person." Take, for instance, a man who unexplainably survives a car accident. While this experience evokes deep gratitude and strengthens his faith in God, he nevertheless feels uneasy when friends say, "God rescued you." His unease stems from his concern that a theistic conception of God as a person makes God appear to be arbitrary and capricious. For if God rescued him, why did God not rescue countless thousands of others who died in auto accidents that year? So, his unambiguous gratefulness is directed instead to the illimitable Mystery of God, whose ways vastly outstrip our human capacity to fully understand.

Thus, Steindl-Rast distinguishes between "personal gratitude" which "deserves to be called *thankfulness*, because it typically expresses itself in thanks given to the giver by the receiver of the gift" and "transpersonal gratitude" which "deserves to be called *gratefulness*, because it is typically the full response of a person to gratuitous belonging."[30] We experience transpersonal gratitude at intense moments when we sense that we have been gracefully touched, somehow, by the mysterious presence of the divine. Douglas Steere, a prolific writer on prayer and the spiritual life in the Quaker tradition, describes such moments as fingers that point to the Presence.

> Who has never felt melted down and brought to tears of tenderness at a great passage in a book, a scene in a play, a sight of the sea, a word or the hug of a child, a surge of pain, a midnight hour in a 'white night' when we have been shown the way and have yielded, or at one of those moments in a conversation with a friend where we touched "where words come from?"

These minor ecstasies...are fingers. They all point to the Presence.[31]

Further illustration of these peak moments that lead naturally to gratefulness can be seen in the following two accounts. Bernard Berenson recalls a time when he lost himself in "some instant of perfect harmony."

> In childhood and boyhood this ecstasy overtook me when I was happy out of doors. Was I five or six? Certainly not seven. It was morning in early summer. A silver haze shimmered and trembled over the lime trees. The air was laden with their fragrance. The temperature was like a caress. I remember—I need not recall—that I climbed up a tree stump and felt suddenly immersed in Itness. I did not call it by that name. I had no need for words. It and I were one.[32]

Admiral Byrd's description of his 1934 experience in the Antarctic provides another vivid illustration of what Steindl-Rast is pointing to when he speaks of gratefulness.

> Took my daily walk at 4 p.m. today in eighty-nine degrees of frost....I paused to listen to the silence.... The day was dying, the night being born—but with great peace. Here were imponderable processes and forces of the cosmos, harmonious and soundless. Harmony, that was it!...
>
> It was enough to catch that rhythm, momentarily to be part of it. In that instant I could feel no doubt of man's [sic] oneness with the universe. The conviction came that the rhythm was too orderly, too harmonious, too perfect to be a product of blind chance—that, therefore, there must be purpose in the whole

and that man [sic] was part of that whole and not an accidental off-shoot. It was a feeling that transcended reason; that went to the heart of man's [sic] despair and found it groundless.[33]

When people like Berenson and Byrd experience such an intense oneness and harmony in the universe, they are typically flooded with a profound gratefulness.

To describe gratefulness as "mystical" or to link it with "peak experiences" is not to assert that it is an experience accessible to only special kinds of people, like the more creative, imaginative, artistic, or spiritual personalities among us. Rather, as Maslow noted clearly in his study of self-actualizing people, "Peak experiences are far more common than I had expected…I now suspect they occur in practically everybody although without being recognized or accepted for what they are."[34] Maslow wrote that the people he studied reported "having had something like mystic experiences…I gave up the name 'mystic' experience and started calling them peak experiences."[35] Typically, these experiences make us "feel lucky, fortunate, graced." During and after peak experiences, people react with a sense that "I don't deserve this" and consequently feel grateful to God or to fate, nature, or just good fortune. The spiritual challenge, according to Steindl-Rast, is "to recognize our mystical moments and to accept them for what they are…truly religious experiences" which naturally direct our gaze to God in gratitude and love. As he nicely puts it, "A mystic is not a special kind of human being; rather, every human being is a special kind of mystic— potentially, at least…We can realize our mystic potential through grateful living."[36] Clearly, gratitude as thankfulness (as described by positive psychologists) and gratitude as gratefulness (as described by Steindl-Rast) are two important components of a spirituality of gratitude. While the empirical findings of positive psychologists encourage us to grow in giving thanks to all who benefit us, Steindl-Rast's reflections invite us to stay open to being struck by amazement at the gratuity of everything that surrounds us.

❧ SPIRITUAL EXERCISES AND REFLECTIONS ❧

Gratitude as a spiritual pathway entails the regular use of practices that can keep us alert and aware of the blessings and gifts of our life. Whether done daily, weekly, or monthly, concrete practices keep us from slipping into taking things for granted and thereby strengthen our disposition for gratitude. The following are some simple gratitude practices:

Breathing with Gratitude

Occasionally throughout the day, slow down to pay attention to your breathing. Notice how this vital process of inhaling and exhaling happens so naturally, sustaining our aliveness, moment by moment.

Let your attention to your breathing remind you of the blessing of being alive and well. Let it stir up feelings of gratitude to God, for it is in God that we live and breathe, and move, and have our being.

Reliving a Blessed Moment of the Day

Before retiring at night, briefly scan the activities and happenings, encounters and conversations you experienced that day. What brought you a moment of joy, excitement, pleasure, relaxation, or sense of well-being? These can be simple things we often take for granted: a morning cup of coffee in quiet solitude or with someone we feel close to; a kindness extended to us by a stranger on our commute to work; a phone conversation that re-connected us with someone we miss; a kind word of concern or affirmation from a colleague, neighbor, or friend; a short break during the day that restored our energy and lifted our spirit.

Focus on just one such gratitude-evoking experience. In your memory and imagination, recall and relive this moment, letting your appreciation and gratitude for it deepen.

This kind of gratitude review can surprise us with how often we let small, but significant, blessings slip through the cracks, not allowing them to fuel gratefulness in our hearts.

Recalling Our Blessings Regularly

Because of the human tendency to become habituated to the many gifts and blessings we enjoy, it is important to call them to mind regularly, whether in a gratitude journal or in prayer. As Garrison Keillor of *The Prairie Home Companion* states, "List your blessings and you will walk through those gates of thanksgiving and into the fields of joy." In an informal prayer of thanksgiving, Keillor gives us a good example of how to address God in intimate and familial terms:

> Thank you, Lord, for giving me the wherewithal not to fix a half-pound cheeseburger right now and to eat a stalk of celery instead. Thank you for the wonderful son and the amazing daughter and the smart sexy wife and the grandkids....Thank you for the odd delight of being sixty, part of which is the sheer relief of not being fifty. I could go on and on....[37]

Prayers of thanksgiving can be formal ones that we have learned, like a traditional grace before meals, or an informal one that springs spontaneously from our heart.

CHAPTER 2

Gratitude as
the Echo of Grace

Grace names the ways in which we find favor with God
and one another, the surprising ways in which we
know ourselves to be blessed.

—JAMES AND EVELYN WHITEHEAD[1]

THE BENEFITS OF GRATITUDE are not restricted to those who possess religious faith, but are enjoyed by people who simply count
their blessings. However, having faith or a spiritual outlook contributes greatly to an attitude of gratitude, as positive psychologists have discovered in their study of the disposition for
gratitude. Christian spirituality understands gratitude as more
than a transient feeling; it is an abiding vision that recognizes
the gift-nature of everything. William C. Spohn, the late moral
theologian and our good friend, captured this understanding
when he spoke of gratitude as "the echo of grace." Like an echo,
gratitude reverberates in our hearts when the gratuity of everything dawns on us.

Bill's articulation of this insight into gratitude is particularly poignant in its timing. In Holy Week of 2004, while consult-
ing for the Lilly Endowment in Indianapolis, he suffered
seizures that scrambled his speech and landed him in the hospital. This sudden intrusion of illness led to a diagnosis of brain

cancer and then death at age sixty-one, after a relatively short period of treatment. During this time, those of us who received his e-mail updates were given a final gift from this brilliant and faith-filled man. In his last days, Bill shared with us his experience of God's graciousness and the gratitude that issues forth from deep faith. In his first post-surgery e-mail, he expressed gratefulness for the experience of God's healing love being part of his circle of friends. "We have found that God's love and healing are not add-ons: your support has been not only the sign of God's grace, but the principal way it has come to us."[2] Later, during the course of treatment, he shared:

> We experience much gratitude, which is the echo of grace. Illness can bog one down in self-absorption. Your support helps open the windows for grace, which comes through many channels, the major one being friends, but also wonderful spouses, talented surgeons, radiologists with good aim, and insightful therapists. I don't believe that God sends tumors to anyone, but we have found that on our brief walk through the valley of darkness, God has certainly been with us.[3]

Bill's thoughtful enumeration of people for whom he was grateful reveals the density that characterized his grateful disposition. His faith enabled him to sense the loving approach of God in the people who surrounded him. Throughout this "walk through the valley of darkness," his wife Martha Stortz, professor of historical theology and ethics at Pacific Lutheran Theological Seminary, also manifested a grateful disposition. Sharing her experience of the emotional roller-coaster ride of living through Bill's regimen of surgeries, radiation, scans, and chemotherapy, she confessed that at one point, she "begged a neighbor, 'If you see my Old Life wandering down the street, please send it back!'"

However, she continued, "the New Life had its graces. At the end of each day we recounted them and fell asleep grateful."[4]

Using the language of faith, Bill gave us a precious lesson about how faith fosters gratitude. "We use the language available to us from our tradition," he wrote. "However, it does not seem an artificial imposition but the articulation of the core of what is going on."[5] In a poignant account of his experience of imminent death, Bill shared this final testimony of faith: "The last six months have been nothing like I feared the encounter with death would be. We are not called to summon up a great act of hope, but to turn our attention to the One who is faithful. As a professional student, I guess I imagined that this would be the ultimate final exam, and I'd better get it right." Instead, with marvel and gratitude, he discovered "that there is more gift than accomplishment in all of this. If gratitude is the echo of grace, then hope is the echo of God's paying attention to us."[6]

Bill's faith led him to distinguish between resignation and surrender. Resignation feels like "This is just the way it is, so 'tough it out,' " he wrote, while surrender "is not giving up, but saying 'Into Your hands I commend my spirit, O Lord.' "[7] Surrender was not always easy, he admits: "There are times when there isn't much energy for surrender and then it seems more like resignation. But fortunately those times are rare...." In the end, Bill summed up beautifully what enabled him to surrender in trust. While he realized that some people could chalk up his attitude of faith to "deep reservoirs of denial," he adamantly differed.

> Our thoughts are somewhat different. Who knows, "God's ways" may be surprisingly better than the scripture of Kubler-Ross and all the other gurus of grief. Yes, there are undeniable losses, but they don't compare with the advent of God's approach. In the original context of Isaiah, "God's ways" refers to a goodness

that takes our breath away. Most of this is not mystical or abstract. It comes in very concrete ways, primarily through other people.[8]

FAITH FOSTERS GRATITUDE

While Bill's Christian faith took root as a child growing up in a religious Irish-German family, the single most significant impact on his faith formation as an adult came from the Spiritual Exercises of St. Ignatius.[9] As a Jesuit for thirty-two years, Bill made the full thirty-day Spiritual Exercises twice, once when he first entered the Jesuits in 1962 and again years later after his ordination as a priest. Besides these two experiences, he followed the Jesuit practice of making an annual eight-day retreat based on the Ignatian Exercises. The long years of Jesuit formation "had done more to shape my life as a Christian than any peak experience," he once wrote, for "the values and mindset of Jesus only gradually enter into character over a lifetime."[10] His vigorous life of faith, as well as the lives of countless others throughout history, testifies to the tremendous power of the Spiritual Exercises to cultivate a lively Christian faith. In this chapter, we discuss how Ignatius of Loyola's sixteenth-century classic, *The Spiritual Exercises*, can facilitate an experience of spiritual transformation by deepening our faith in God's love and by expanding our awareness of how richly we have been blessed by a good and giving God.

The Spiritual Exercises: Shaping Grateful Hearts

The *Spiritual Exercises* represents Ignatius' attempt to objectivize his own experience in order to share the graces that he himself received.[11] They are structured according to four "weeks." Like the seven "days" of creation, the Ignatian "weeks" are not to be taken literally as seven calendar days, but rather as a way of structuring the various matter for prayer throughout the process. The First Week focuses on how our human sinfulness and struggles are met with the gift of God's merciful and forgiving love. The following three weeks focus on the love of God made manifest in the life, death, and resurrection of Jesus. The four "weeks" are sandwiched between two meditations that serve as bookends: the "First Principle and Foundation" at the beginning of the Exercises and the "Contemplation to Attain Love" at the end of the four week experience. Moving from one "week" to the next depends on whether the retreatant has received the grace sought in that particular "week." These graces will be delineated below.

Throughout the four "weeks" of the Exercises, Ignatius traces out for us how the love of God has unfolded in salvation history, and, in so doing, moves us to a deeper and deeper insight into the love of God. Step by step, Ignatius illustrates the progressive manifestation of divine love, starting with creation and ending with God's restoration of abundant life in the resurrection of Jesus. At a time when ecological spiritualities are responding to our environmental crisis by placing a much-needed focus on God's love, shown in creating and sustaining the cosmos, the Ignatian vision provides balance. It reminds us that "while the loving presence of God in creation remains a constant, [creation]...is not God's full or final word of love."[12] Those making the Exercises contemplate the love of God expressed in multiple ways: in the creation of the world, in the ongoing preservation of our life, in the incarnation of the divine Word and in the life, death, and resurrection of Jesus.

Gratitude: The Central Motif of the Spiritual Exercises

Gratitude is a central theme in the *Spiritual Exercises*.[13] This is most clearly seen when we look at the structure of the final meditation, the Contemplation to Attain Love, through which Ignatius attempts to deepen our love of God by expanding our sense of God's generosity to us. When we review the four points of the Contemplation to Attain Love, it is evident how Ignatius meant them to be avenues to gratitude.

- *Everything is gift.* This first consideration invites us to contemplate the gifts of creation and redemption, and the special blessings and favors we have personally received. We note here that the gratitude span suggested for our consideration integrates gratitude for God's love manifested in the marvels of creation, as well as God's love made known in the sacrificial love of Jesus. We are also asked to dwell on how we have been concretely and personally blessed.

- *God dwells intimately in all God's gifts.* This second reflection reminds us that God not only is the creator of life and the giver of gifts, but also dwells in all created things, especially in the human person, the *imago Dei.* In other words, God not only gives us gifts, but offers the gift of God's Self.

- *God's love is actively at work on our behalf.* This third consideration asserts that God's presence in the world is not inert, but dynamic: God labors for us in all of creation.

- *God is the Loving Source, From Whom All Blessings Flow.* Finally, the fourth point of the Contemplation portrays all of God's blessings as descending from above—like water from a fountain or rays from the sun.

Gratitude is clearly the heart of this final meditation. Furthermore, Ignatian scholars have argued that it is a summarizing meditation that recaps the whole experience, because the four considerations closely correspond to the four weeks of the Exercises. Thus, gratitude can be said to permeate the entire experience.[14]

GRATITUDE: THE THRESHOLD TO LOVING SERVICE

Ignatius intended the Spiritual Exercises to be a transformative process, in which we would be so moved with gratitude for God's bountiful goodness that the resulting love would evoke a generous desire to give in return. Thus, he suggests that we pray for the following desire: "Here it will be to ask for an intimate knowledge of the many blessings received, that filled with gratitude for all, I may in all things love and serve the Divine Majesty."[15] Reflected in this petition is a three-fold movement—from "intimate knowledge" to gratitude, and from gratitude to love, which is expressed in service. The dynamic begins with considering how we have been gifted by God, not only in a global fashion, but in concrete and particular ways.[16] Awareness of the many blessings of God easily arouses our gratitude and brings us to a stance of humble thanksgiving. Ignatius hoped that this deepening gratitude would be shown in free and loving service.[17] In short, the full goal sought in contemplating God's goodness consists in a unity of three moments—interior knowledge, love, and action.

Bill Spohn's responses to the ups and downs of cancer treatment revealed how profoundly he was shaped by this Ignatian ideal of gratitude flowing into service. After a second surgery left him with "a string of seahorse-shaped sutures and an impressive incision above my left ear from which I will try to protect the faint of heart," Bill reflected, "Life is not a private investment account where we get back what we paid in; rather, others give life to us freely, and we pass that gift on to still others."[18] To illustrate this point, Spohn shared the story of his young doctor.

> Our neuro-oncologist is a brilliant young doctor who went to a Jesuit grammar school at Gesu Parish in inner-city Detroit. He told us that people change your life, but sometimes institutions do too. This grammar school set him on the path of his calling. The people who taught him gave away their formation freely, and now he's giving his knowledge and dedication freely to his patients. He can't pay back the original debt, but he pays it forward to people whom the Gesu community will never meet. Somehow this is a cameo of the gracious web of life we are all in.[19]

GRACES AS GATEWAYS TO GRATITUDE

Another angle of vision that highlights the centrality of gratitude in the Spiritual Exercises comes from looking at the graces sought at each phase of the experience. So that we might grow in gratitude, each part of the Exercises points to a God who is both good and giving, and invites us to a greater mindfulness of the abundant graces of God. A brief elaboration of the graces sought in each phase of the experience makes clear that Ignatius viewed felt-gratitude as pivotal to spiritual transformation.

Grace of the First Principle and Foundation: We Are Desired into Being and Wondrously Made.

This first consideration of the Spiritual Exercises fosters gratitude for the gifts of creation and one's personal life. Each of us has been created in "lone nativities,"[20] not in twos or thousands. The existence we enjoy results from God's conscious love, choosing us to be. Because we are "desired into being,"[21] our basic attitude towards God should be one of gratitude and praise (Rom 1:21). Furthermore, the gift of life is embellished with the gift of a loving relationship with God that is meant to be enjoyed in the "here-and-now" and in the "hereafter."

The First Principle and Foundation meditation invites us to view life as a journey or pilgrimage. We come from God and are meant to return to God, the source and fulfillment of our existence. Inspired by an image suggested by Julian of Norwich, a contemporary theologian captures poetically this faith vision embedded in the First Principle and Foundation, when she says, "Desire is the great seal on our souls, marking where we have been 'oned' with God in the instant of our creation." And even when our earthly sojourn has caused us to wander far from this "precious oneing," "desire is the beautiful, scathing brand that reminds us who we are and to whom we belong."[22] These sentiments echo Augustine' cry that "You have made us for yourself, O God, and our hearts will remain restless, until they rest in you." Our hearts long for a love that will abide beyond death.

Bill Spohn's peaceful acceptance of death marked him as a person who had embraced the truth of Ignatius' view of life. In his last e-mail update in May 2005, he shared the sad news that the doctors had confirmed that the tumor had once again grown back, or, in one doctor's words, "Clearly, you failed the trial drug." His wife Marty describes the immediate events that led to Bill's final "Yes" to God's call to return to the loving source from which he came.[23]

> We had the scan Thursday a week ago, then met with the surgeon the following day at 9 a.m. He would give us the first read on the scan. We had to drive into the city during rush hour, so we read the lessons for the day before tackling the traffic. The text was John 21:15–19, the passage where Jesus questions Peter again and again: "Do you love me?" After Peter's repeated profes-

sions of love, Jesus says to him: "When you were younger, you used to fasten your own belt and go wherever you wished. But when you grow old, you will stretch out your hands, and someone else will fasten a belt around you and take you where you do not wish to go. Follow me." It was hard driving across the Bay Bridge with that text in our hearts. But we got to the city early and went up to St. Ignatius Church on the USF campus. Always we were drawn to the side chapel and to St. Ignatius' *Suscipe* on the wall. The first part of that prayer is a pretty accurate description of brain cancer, and that terrified us both, but the second part offered the consolation we craved:

Take, Lord, receive all my liberty,
my memory, my understanding,
and my entire will,
All that I am and call my own.

You have given it all to me.
To you, Lord, I return it.
Everything is yours, do with it what you will.

Give me only your love and your grace.
That is enough for me.

In the end, this prayerful surrender to a beckoning and loving God reflected the faith that shaped Bill's lifelong disposition of gratitude. Because of that *Suscipe* prayer, he wrote to his friends, "We were ready when the surgeon told us the tumor had grown back. And we were ready when he said the chemo had not been working. We are living inside that prayer. All things considered, it is not a bad place to be. You are part of this journey more than you know. The love that we experience through you not only helps us along the way, but is already the beginning of the abundant life to come." Clearly, Ignatius' First Principle and Foundation left a lasting imprint on Bill's soul.

Grace of the First Week:
Though Sinful, We Are Loved Unconditionally.

In the First Week, we seek a felt-knowledge both of our sinfulness and God's merciful love that keeps us in an accepting embrace—no matter how we have faltered and sinned. Ignatius hoped that the experience of the First Week would sear in our consciousness that "the once-and-for-all forgiveness that Christians celebrate…[is] not something that happens within God but something that happens within us when we become aware of the impossibility of turning God away from us, so precious are we to God. We are united with the erotic power that is God. This is our nature and nothing can change or undo that unity."[24] The grace of the First Week has taken firm root, when we can acknowledge our failings with unshakable confidence in the constancy of God. Deep within, we know that we are loved sinners.

Luke's three parables in chapter fifteen, his "lost and found department," capture the spirit of the First Week, which celebrates the unconditional love of God. The parables of the lost sheep, the lost coin, and the prodigal son drive home the point that God's love for us endures—no matter how we have sinned and lost our way. According to Jesus, God can be likened to a shepherd who, having a hundred sheep and losing one, leaves the ninety-nine in search of the one lost sheep. The shepherd's decision defies normal business sense that would suggest that someone in that situation should "cut their losses" by either building better fences or hiring more help to watch over the flock. In the second parable in chapter fifteen, Jesus compares God to a woman who has lost a coin that she greatly values. She turns her whole house upside down in search of this coin. And when she finds it, she throws a party to celebrate. When we identify with being the lost coin and imagine God's loving attachment to us, like that of the woman for her coin, we get the point of Jesus' message—we are precious in God's eyes and recipients of God's lavish love. The final parable in this triplet is that of the story of the prodigal son, so richly portrayed in Rembrandt's *Return of the Prodigal Son*, housed in the Hermitage Museum in St. Petersburg. This richly textured story weaves together so many strands of the Good News proclaimed by Jesus: that we can always go home, no matter how badly we have failed to achieve our goals; that we live in a multiple-chance universe and are never doomed by past mistakes; that God allows for trial-and-error learning; and finally that our sometimes tortuous return will always be met by a loving God, who like the "prodigal father" celebrates with exuberant joy, because "this son of mine was lost and is now found, was dead and has come back to life." Each of the three parables ends with a joyful celebration. Similarly, the First Week's consideration of sin is meant to end with joy and consolation. These parables contain the heart of Jesus' message: God's love for us is not only extravagant, but also constant. It is a love that far outstrips human norms of fairness and contradicts the rules of common sense.

As a theologian, Bill Spohn appreciated the importance of Jesus' parables. Parables were used by Jesus to shape our consciousness—so that we might perceive reality more and more as Jesus did and to react to events and people like he did. "Jesus used parables" he once wrote, "to shock his audience into recognizing that their ways were not God's ways."[25] Through his life of prayer and experience of the Spiritual Exercises over the years, Bill clearly internalized the grace of the First Week. He believed in the constancy of God's love throughout our many meanderings in life. It was this faith that enabled him to make a life-giving, though risk-filled, change at mid-life—a change that was harder for him than suffering from brain cancer. Once again, his wife Marty relates his experience with sensitive love:

> Radiation ended around the Feast of the Transfiguration. We joked that Bill's face was glowing, too, and made plans to spend a week at Monterey Bay. The ocean calmed us: We could look beyond the frantic surface action of the waves to a horizon that never changed. It was a metaphor for the spiritual journey. Bill's 32 years as a Jesuit served us both well. It offered ways of naming consolation we experienced. Indeed, his hardest trial was not brain cancer. That August he wrote to a friend and fellow classmate in the Society of Jesus, "Leaving the Society was far more fearful than this. I didn't know who I would be, whether my family and friends would still stand by me, whether I could do the work I had trained to do, and whether God would still take my calls. Perhaps having found that all those fears were pointless, this experience is not fearful. I know that I will not be abandoned.[26]

Besides personal sin, the First Week also includes reflecting on our collective sinfulness and the harm it has caused in the world. By reflecting on humankind's sinful past—"man's inhumanity to man"—we humbly admit that our sinfulness has caused things to happen in the world that are stunning reversals of God's intent for creation. The world as we have it is not the best we can hope for, nor the world God intends, but a badly broken and disordered one. Our prayer during this First Week of the retreat also entails asking for the desire, motivated by gratitude for the gift of God's forgiving love, to work with Christ to restore order and harmony to the created universe. The Kingdom mediation that follows extends Christ's invitation to intimate collaboration.

Grace of the Call of the King Meditation: We Are Called to Be Participants in God's Project on Earth.

As a transition between the First and Second Weeks, this meditation focuses on the gift of covenant partnership, i.e. that each of us has been called to share in God's work in the world today. Situated immediately after the First Week, it is psychologically intended to maximize our gratitude: feelings of gratitude are still lingering in our hearts for the grace of forgiveness received in the First Week, when Ignatius has us consider that we are also chosen to collaborate with God. The grace of the Kingdom meditation is a heartfelt gratitude that our sinfulness does not disqualify us from serving along side Jesus in intimate collaboration, as friends and coworkers.[27] But, like Peter who betrayed Jesus, we are called in our weakness and limitations. A central purpose of the Spiritual Exercises is to help each of us to discern how this call is to take particular form in the concrete reality of our life. We ask, for example, "How am I being called—in the here and now—to contribute to God's project on earth, given my unique personality, talents, and background?" Because of the fluidity and multiple transitions of life, as well as increased longevity, we must ask this question throughout the different seasons of life.

Educated in a Jesuit high school where Ignatian retreats were regularly scheduled events, Spohn's life-choices were naturally framed by Ignatius' Kingdom meditation. Upon graduating from St. Ignatius College Preparatory in San Francisco in 1962, Bill followed what he discerned was God's call—to join the Jesuits with the goal of serving as priest. In the course of his early formation, he further discerned that he was being called to contribute to the Kingdom of God as a moral theologian. This led to graduate studies at the University of Chicago and later at its divinity school. As fellow moral theologian Anne E. Patrick recounts, Bill's discernment of God's call near the end of his life took the form of a concrete academic project. She writes

> At the time he was first stricken with symptoms of brain cancer in April 2004, Bill Spohn was working on a book that would trace American thinkers from Jonathan Edwards through H. Richard Niebuhr as a source for a distinctively American moral theology. He wanted to overcome the limitations he found in much revisionist moral theology, especially that of German Jesuits who, to Spohn's mind, combined insights from Rahner and Kant in a way that was strong on universality but weak on Christian distinctiveness and inspirational force.[28]

Because Bill was someone shaped by the Spiritual Exercises, it is safe to conjecture that the Kingdom meditation influenced his vocational choices throughout life.

Bill's sense of the importance of detecting the call of God in all situations illuminates what he shared when his cancer forced life-style changes. Lamenting the "unintended asceticism" illness brought, he made the following reflection:

> It is surprising that even limitations contain a calling and invitation. Life has gotten more contemplative because there is more time and less driving energy. A number of things that seemed important before don't anymore. Does the world really need any more footnote-choked articles and dense presentations at conferences? The few things that are important have been enormously more important: love in all its forms, the one we married, family, friends old and new, a fine university to work at, the community of faith in its universal reach. T. S. Elliot articulates the prayer of "Ash

Wednesday" and all of life's Lents: "Teach us to care and not to care/ Teach us to sit still."[29]

Grace of the Second Week: Fostering Intimacy with Jesus.

The Second Week consists in contemplating the hidden life and public ministry of Jesus. Our desire here is to acquire an intimate knowledge of Jesus for the sake of a closer walk with Jesus as modern disciples or, as expressed in a song from the musical *Godspell*, our desire is "To see thee more clearly / Love thee more dearly / Follow thee more nearly / Day by day." Ignatius hoped that familiarity with Jesus through prayer would mold us into being more Christ-like in our perceptions and dispositions. The Second Week fosters gratitude for the gift of Jesus, the compassionate love of God made flesh. We are asked to witness how Christ embodies God's compassion to all. Our essential calling as Christians, no matter what our work or career, is to continue Christ's mission by embodying God's compassionate love for those in our life. Ignatius hoped that Christ's compassionate love would stir up our gratitude and draw us to loving service in union with him. As Spohn states, Ignatius

> ...believed that the human desire to serve echoes the divine compassion, that [our] concern for healing the world in our small arena of job and family and community stems from God's desire to heal the world. He wanted people to find where their deepest desires would lead them to serve, because he believed that would be the place where they would find God, or rather, where God would find them.[30]

Grace of the Third Week:
God's Love Manifested in Pain.

The purpose of contemplating the events of Jesus' passion and death during the Third Week is to strengthen our appreciation of how deeply we are loved by God. Hopefully, our gratitude increases as we reflect on Jesus' sacrificial love, a love demonstrated in a trusting surrender to God's will, even to the point of a painful death. Addressing God as *Abba* (an Aramaic term that conveys the intimacy of "papa" or "daddy"), Jesus' faith in God's reliability enabled him to overcome his fear and to pray, "Everything is possible for you. Take this cup away from me. But let it be as you, not I, would have it" (Mark 14:36–37).

We detect resonances of this Gethsemane prayer in an e-mail, in which Bill shared:

> Sometimes it seems like the last three months have been a combination of a retreat and a fairly major hangover. Most times there is a clarity and poignancy about much small and large, and most about the affection that our friends have shown us. There is grieving and gratitude, anxiety but more fundamentally a sense of trust in a benevolent reality "in whom we live and move and have our being." The words of Scripture, especially the psalms, seem less hyperbole and more the unvarnished truth of our condition. This probably won't last, but we will be changed whether it does or not.

Because Ignatius viewed the love of God as ideally what motivates Christian service, his emphasis in the Third Week contemplations of Christ's passion and death is on the love of God manifested in pain. Unlike theories of atonement and satisfaction, the Ignatian approach focuses on love and gratitude, not on repayment and redemption.

Ignatius hoped that a deepened appreciation of God's love would confirm our discernment, made in Week Two, about how God is calling us to serve. Witnessing Jesus' faithful perseverance to his call in the midst of suffering, Ignatius hoped, would strengthen our resolve to serve, even if it involved hardships and struggles. Even though all that we possess has been given to us by God, nothing is required of us in return. Genuine love never demands reciprocation. We do not owe God anything. Nevertheless, love urges us on to an intimate mutuality with a God who loves us so abundantly.[31]

In sum, affective awareness of God's gracious love generates gratitude, which, for Ignatius, serves as a springboard to loving service. This Ignatian approach makes good psychological sense, as a recent investigation into whether gratitude and indebtedness are distinct emotional states makes clear. Concluding that "gratitude and indebtedness may best be viewed as distinct emotional states," the researchers state: "If gifts are given for the purpose of receiving return favours from the beneficiary, the beneficiary is less likely to feel grateful, and is less likely to feel like returning the favour. The more a benefit is received as a gift of grace, the more likely there will be a return of gratitude."[32]

Grace of the Fourth Week: The Gift of New Life to Be Shared by All.

The Fourth Week's focus on the resurrection of Jesus fosters gratitude for God's faithfulness in raising Jesus from the dead and for the reassurance given to us that wherever we experience death, in whatever form, God promises to bring new life, just as God did for Jesus. During the Fourth Week, we ask for the grace to experience the consoling presence of the Risen Jesus, who addresses us now as he did his early disciples: "It is I; do not be afraid" (John 6:20). Like Mary Magdalene's surprising encounter with Christ whom she mistook for the gardener, we are encouraged to receive the consolation of Christ in the midst of our experiences of sadness and loss. Like the disillusioned and hopeless disciples on the way to Emmaus, we are encouraged to discover the Risen Jesus' support in strangers we encounter on the road and in communities in which we share table-fellowship and meaning. And like the re-commissioned Peter, who forfeited his call through his triple denial, we are invited to experience a Risen Christ who graciously restores our relationship with him, no matter how we may have let him down. Like these early followers of Jesus, we are invited to enjoy with gratitude the abiding, peace-filled presence of the Risen Jesus.

The Grace of the Contemplation to Attain Love: All Is Gift.

This final exercise fosters gratitude by inviting us to recall all of God's gifts of creation and redemption and to rejoice in God's loving presence and action in all of reality for us.

GRATITUDE: THE ECHO OF GRACE

The graces received throughout the Spiritual Exercises call for a grateful response. As theologian Karl Barth so aptly remarked, "grace and gratitude go together like heaven and Earth; grace evokes gratitude like the voice an echo."[33] Ignatius felt strongly that gratitude should be the basic response to God's abounding love. Ingratitude, he once wrote, "is the most abominable of all sins, and it is to be detested in the sight of the Creator and Lord by all of God's creatures for it is the forgetting of the graces, benefits and blessings received."[34] To counteract this kind of forgetting, Ignatius asks us in the first point of the Contemplation to Attain Love to recall the many blessings of creation and redemption that we have enjoyed. Recognition of the graces of each week of the Exercises is meant to evoke an ever deepening gratitude for all that we have received. For Ignatius, asking for what we want in prayer is an effective way of shaping our perceptions; when we voice our desires in prayer, God hears us and we hear ourselves. The graces of the Exercises correspond to the desires that Ignatius encourages us to pray for throughout the experience.[35] When we sense on the level of "*sentir*" or felt-knowledge that we have received what we have asked for, we feel favored by God and grateful. Thus, for Ignatius, graces are gateways to gratitude when they are deeply felt and acknowledged.

The Pedagogy of Ignatius

There is a vital difference between knowing something in a conceptual or notional way and knowing it in a heart-felt and affective way. Jesuit Anthony de Mello tells a story that illustrates the difference.

Uwais the Sufi was once asked,
"What has grace brought you?"

He replied,
"When I wake in the morning I feel
like a man who is not sure he will
live till evening."

Said the questioner,
"But doesn't everyone know this?"

Said Uwais,
"They certainly do.

> But not all of them
> feel it."

De Mello concludes, "No one ever became drunk on the word *wine*."[36] Emotional realization is what makes a difference in spiritual transformation. Clearly, Bill Spohn's life of prayer and experience of the Spiritual Exercises gave him an intimate and experiential knowledge of his faith. "Bill talked about Jesus as if they'd just had drinks the night before," his wife Marty recalls. "The freshness and urgency of his message was quite simply infectious. We all wanted to have been there."[37] Because his faith was so deeply felt, Bill was able to teach us by example how to live and how to die with grateful love. Marty poignantly testifies to this, when she shares:

> Bill's best scholarly work was his last one: his reflec-
> tions on his illness in a regular series of e-mails to his
> friends. When he could no longer write, he dictated.
> When he could no longer dictate, he simply lived out
> his message to the last breath. And the message was
> this: "We are not in free fall; everything we believe in
> is true."[38]

Throughout the *Spiritual Exercises,* Ignatius seeks to cultivate deeply-felt knowledge that could stir up gratitude and love. For him, transformation entails internalizing the fullness of God's love in all its manifestations. Ignatius envisions the Spiritual Exercises as an experience to enter, not something to be watched. To distance oneself from the process and to study it only speculatively is to subvert its purpose. Ignatius intends it to be a transformative encounter in which God deals directly and uniquely with each person.[39] The kind of profound interior change sought by Ignatius requires the internalization of the truths of faith through personal exploration and discovery. Thus, he warns the director of the Exercises to refrain from explaining the material at too great a length that could engender passivity. More fruit is gained when we ourselves come to a deep, interior grasp of the matter through self-activity and personal experience, "for it is not much knowledge that fills and satisfies the soul, but the intimate understanding and relish of the truth."[40] Based on his experience of God's forming him, like a schoolmaster treats a child, Ignatius created the Spiritual Exercises as a way by which we could be similarly formed by God.

GOD'S GENEROSITY EVOKES OUR GRATITUDE

Ignatius' focus on the bountifulness of grace enveloping all aspects of our lives is true to the message of Jesus. While Jesus was not a priest in the sense of a cultic official, his "priestliness," according to theologian James Whitehead, was rooted in his witness to the abundance of grace, which he announced wherever he appeared.

> His listeners were, like us, accustomed to the many barriers to and restrictions on God's abundance. Being a foreigner, a tax collector, a woman, a sinner— all these severely jeopardized one's access to God's grace. Religious institutions, then as now, made it their business to control and limit the believer's access to grace. But Jesus insisted that grace was everywhere, overflowing the official channels, available in astonishing abundance.[41]

Jesus consistently proclaimed that God's gracious generosity always gives us more than we dare ask and always outstrips all our norms of human fairness. The following contemporary recasting of the parable of the vineyard laborers (Matt 20:1–16) can give us a renewed appreciation of Jesus' announcement of abundance.

Now the kingdom of heaven, said Jesus, is like a farmer in the Napa valley who went out early at daybreak to find some migrant workers to harvest his grapes. With the forecast of heavy rains, he was anxious to harvest the crop before the ruinous downpour hit. He spotted a small group gathered downtown, at the corner of Main and Juanita, near the freeway exit, and offered to pay them sixty dollars for the day. The men, eager to get started before the temperature heated up, jumped at the chance to get in a full day's wage. A few hours later, while coming out of the bank, the farmer noticed a group of day laborers just sitting around a street corner. He offered them a job with the promise to pay them a fair wage. Having nothing better to do, the men piled into a pick-up and headed out to work in the fields. Then at noon and again at three, the farmer came across more workers, men who had already given up hope of finding work for the day and had settled into a lethargic idleness, partly induced by the dry heat and warm breeze. He was able to motivate them into action by promising to pay them a fair wage. Finally, an hour before quitting time, the farmer recruited a group of eleventh-hour laborers, telling them he'd treat them fairly if they would pitch in.

At day's end, the farmer ordered his foreman to pay the workers, starting with the last arrivals and ending with the first. So those who showed up near the end of the day came forward and received sixty dollars. When the workers who started early at daybreak came, they expected to get more. But they too received sixty dollars. They took the money, but grumbled out loud at the farmer. "The guys who came last," they groused, "only put in an hour. It's not fair to give them the same amount as us, who had to put in a heavy day's work in the hot sun." To one of the complaining workers, the farmer said, "Amigo, I'm not being unjust to you. Didn't I promise to pay you sixty dollars for your day's work? Don't I have the right to pay the last comer as much as I pay you? Why be envious because I'm generous?"

Followers of Jesus become priestly, states Whitehead, when their lives witness to the same abundance proclaimed by Jesus. In modern times, Pope John XXIII stands out as an inspiring example of living with a Christ-like spirit of expansiveness and generosity. The good-natured, roly-poly pontiff was elected to serve as an interim pope, someone who wouldn't rock the boat of Peter with calls for change. Among his colleagues in the College of Cardinals, he was not seen as "a mover and a shaker." Thus, it was quite a surprise when this unassuming, easy-going pope convoked Vatican Council II, which ushered in the most dramatic changes in the Catholic Church in modern times. And it all started with the simple wish of this people-loving pope to better meet the needs of the times by updating the Church. The pope wanted *aggiornamento*, the happy Italian word for "today-ing." No one suspected that when he opened the windows of the Church to let in some fresh air such a huge pentecostal gale would blow in instead. The main purpose of the Vatican II reforms was to continue Jesus' announcement of the abundance of grace.

In his personal life, Pope John also exuded the spirit of generosity described in the parable of the vineyard workers. A delightful example of his graciousness occurred when he was taking a stroll in the papal gardens one bright spring day at the same time an American group was just exiting from the Vatican Museum. A woman from Omaha was so excited at getting an unexpected glimpse of the pontiff that she impulsively broke from her group and approached the pope. Naturally affable, the pope greeted her with a warm smile. "I don't mean to bother you, your Holiness," spouted the wide-eyed woman who was so impressed by the immense size of the Vatican complex, "but, I was just wondering how many people work here." Pope John paused for a second and with a twinkle in his eyes, answered, "Oh, I guess about half."

⟡ SPIRITUAL EXERCISES AND REFLECTIONS ⟡

Cherishing the Gift of Self

For it was you who formed my inward parts;
>   You knit me together in my mother's womb.
I praise you, for I am fearfully and wonderfully
>   made.
>   Wonderful are your works;
that I know very well. (Ps 139:13–14)

According to Ignatius' First Principle and Foundation, our self is the first gift of God to us, for each of us was "desired into being" at the moment of our creation. A grateful life must be rooted in a deep appreciation for the gift of our life and a love of self that makes us turn to God, our loving Source, with gratitude and love.

Grateful acceptance of ourselves is critical to faith, because, as theologian Johannes Metz states, assent to God begins with one's sincere assent to oneself, just as sinful flight from God starts in one's flight from oneself.[42]

Part of receiving the grace of the First Principle and Foundation is the ability to say "yes" to the self that is wondrously and uniquely fashioned by God.

- How would you assess your relationship to yourself?

- Where is there peaceful acceptance and gratitude for who and how you are?

- Where are you challenged to grow in self-acceptance?

Regarding personal limitations:

- Which are rooted in reality and invite your acceptance?

- Which allow for some improvement and invite your efforts to change?

Prayer for Serenity

God, give me the serenity to accept what I cannot change,
The courage to change what I can,
And the wisdom to know the difference. Amen.

Gratitude for the Gift of
Covenant Partnership with God

A central aspect of Ignatian spirituality highlights the invitation to each of us to be partners in God's work in the world. We are invited, like Jesus, to embody God's love and compassion, forgiveness and healing. Discovering how we—with our particular talents and abilities, desires and interests—are uniquely called to serve can lead to a meaningful and grateful life.

- How do you feel drawn to serve God at this time in your life? Or, as poet Mary Oliver poses so provocatively, "What do you plan to do with your one, wild, and precious life?"

- What do your recurrent deep desires point to as concrete ways of partnering up with God, who continues to labor in the world for the good of all humankind? The answer to this question, according to Ignatian spirituality, is a solid indicator of how you are being called to collaborate with God.

CHAPTER 3

Secret to Gratitude—
The Eye of the Beholder

Gratitude *is* the vision—the way of seeing—
That recognizes "gift."[1]

FOSTERING GRATITUDE entails training our perception for a grateful response to life. Our perception, or take on things, is shaped by the lenses through which we view the world. Tourists in large city, for example, who happen upon a crime scene, will notice quite different things than the crime scene investigators, hovering over the site with microscopic alertness. Furthermore, our perception directly influences the way we feel and act. To be grateful, therefore, we need lenses that help us *see* the things and events of ordinary life in a way that evokes gratitude. Christian spirituality supports grateful living by encouraging us to see "through the eyes of faith." "My *experience is what I agree to attend to,*" philosopher William James once noted. "Only those items which I *notice* shape my mind—without selective interest, experience is an utter chaos."[2] Thus, determining what we pay attention to gives us the power to shape what we perceive or, in James' words, the power to "shape my mind." A Christian spirituality of gratitude is rooted in a mind that has been molded by a belief in the active presence of a good and giving God, permeating the whole universe and all of human life.

SCRIPTURE AS AN OPTIC "LENS" TO DETECT GRACE

Stories and events in the Bible can be used as lenses to help us to detect the movements of grace and to recognize how God may be acting in our lives. They can serve as paradigms for perception. In other words, Scripture contains images and patterns that light up areas of our experience. "A paradigm," states theologian Kathleen Fischer, "is an experience which illumines all other experiences, in the light of which its deeper dimensions are revealed."[3] Saying that Scripture is paradigmatic means that scriptural events can serve as patterns of understanding, illuminating events in such a way that our blindness to God's saving presence gives way to insight. "Paradigmatic events, such as the exodus, the exile, and the death/resurrection of Jesus, provide lens through which we can view all the events of human life," states Fischer. "Our access to these events is through the master images by which they become living tradition....It is not so much the images themselves which we know. Rather, we know our life in a new way through them."[4] Scriptural paradigms can help us "see" the connection between how God acted in events narrated in Scripture and how God is similarly acting in our lives. The graced understanding provided by scriptural paradigms thus helps us perceive in a way that evokes gratitude. This is because, "*Paradigms power perception and perceptions power emotions.* Most emotions are responses to perception—what you think is true about a given situation." [5]

Scriptural Paradigms and the Analogical Imagination

Because they convey to us not only what God did in the past, but what God is always doing, biblical paradigms can serve as illuminating references for spiritual insight into our own story. The key is finding the similarity, the analogy between the biblical story and our personal experience. Analogy entails deepening our knowledge of a reality by understanding it in reference to something similar, though not identical. The things being compared have similarities, as well as dissimilarities. When we catch the rhyme between the scriptural narrative and our own story, we are able to see better what God is doing in our life. Instrumental to catching the rhyme is the analogical imagination. "Analogical thinking discovers similarities within difference by recognizing a common pattern within diversity."[6] While the words *fantasy* and *imagination* are sometimes used synonymously, there is a significant distinction between the two. When we fantasize, we turn away from reality; when we imagine, we turn towards reality with eyes of possibility, hope, and deeper understanding. "The task of the imagination," clarifies Bill Spohn, "is to imagine reality and to remake it. Imagination is the opposite of *fantasy*, which fabricates an image to evade reality. Imagination engages particular realities and places them in a context, an intelligible landscape."[7]

Imaginative contemplation of Scripture has been popularized by its predominant use in the Spiritual Exercises of St. Ignatius. Out of a total of 150 prayer periods included in the retreat, 135 involve praying over a scriptural passage through the eyes of the imagination. In praying with a biblical story, we are invited by Ignatian contemplation to move with our imagination and senses directly into the event and relive it as if it were our own experience. When we teach people how to use the method of Ignatian contemplation, we rely on a procedure used by Gestalt therapists when working with dreams. The technique employed in Gestalt dream work contains three steps. First, the client is asked to narrate the contents of the dream, just as he or she would in telling a story or recounting an experience. Second, the client is asked to shift the narrative into the present tense and describe how the dream would be reenacted, as if staging a play and giving directions to actors about how they should position themselves and what they are supposed to be doing and saying. Third, the client is asked to take the part of the different characters or aspects of the dream. This last step invites the client to fully identify with the people and action contained in the dream.

The three-step approach of Gestalt dream work is helpful for someone learning how to do Ignatian contemplation. By applying the same three steps to contemplating a mystery of the Bible, we can achieve a progressively deeper immersion into the mystery of faith. An application of this Gestalt procedure to praying with scripture could take this form:

- First, read the account of an event or mystery, like the cure of the blind beggar Bartimaeus at the end of the Way section in Mark's Gospel (10:46–52).

- Second, identify with one of the onlookers and describe the action from his or her point of view. Do this as if the event were actually unfolding right now in front of your eyes.

- Third, insert yourself into the event by identifying with one of the active participants in the scene. As you experience what is happening in the gospel scene, be aware of what you are thinking, sensing, and feeling— your entire subjective response.

The value of this approach is that it can plunge us so deeply into a gospel mystery that we get caught up in a personal and graced encounter with God, mediated through the inspired words of Scripture. As often happens in a psychodrama or a play, there can come a time in contemplation when the artificiality of the put-on identity slips away and the gospel character comes to life in us. Then, it is no longer, for example, Bartimaeus the blind beggar who is being summoned to Jesus and being healed. It is the blind person in us who is being led out of the darkness of personal confusion by Jesus' healing touch. It is the blind part of us that has lost its way in a valued relationship or a depressed part that is blind to any meaning in life. Then, it is no longer just a study of the historical Jesus interacting with people in biblical times. When our contemplation shifts from imaginative role-playing to spontaneous identification, we are drawn into a graced encounter with the risen Christ today.

Moving us beyond a mere cognitive grasp of Scripture, this immersion allows the gospel event to spring to life and to become a lively happening in which we participate. We are then able to encounter the text in a way that provides personal meaning. The analogical imagination plunges down into the concrete particulars of a biblical story in such a way that the plunge down can generate—through the action of God's Spirit—a surge up into insight. Through grace, we experience an "aha moment" when we realize how the biblical account of God's graceful action in the past parallels what God is doing in our life today. In his book that discusses the relation between the New Testament and ethics, Spohn provides a succinct summary of the value of contemplating Scripture through the method of identification with Gospel characters:

> As we tangibly and visually move into their narrated encounter with the Lord, we find in ourselves some echo of their response: If Peter could be forgiven, so can I. If the father could welcome home the prodigal son, then my fears of God's anger are without foundation. We learn to "ask for what we want" in these contemplations by the example of these characters in the story. They raise our expectations and open us to hear the Lord's word to us today.[8]

By helping us spot the similarities that exist between biblical narratives and our own experiences, Ignatian contemplation moves us from the memory of God's intervention in the past to a perception of divine intervention in the present. It trains our imagination to catch the "rhyme" that can be revelatory of grace at work in our lives today.

Detecting Grace Through Scriptural Lenses

The illustrations that follow are designed to show how scriptural paradigms work as lenses of perception, enhancing our gratitude by opening our eyes to the traces of grace that weave, often unnoticed, throughout our life and enabling us to be eye-witnesses to grace at work on our behalf.

Death and Resurrection

Without doubt, the central paradigm of Christian faith is the death and resurrection of Jesus. When God reached into the tomb and raised Jesus from the dead, divine Mystery revealed itself as the One who always brings new life from death and the One for whom nothing is impossible. Christians are called to view everything in life from the perspective of the paschal mystery, which assures us that wherever we experience death or diminishment, God will be there to bring forth new life. Jesus summarized the paschal pattern of life in a verse: "Unless a grain of wheat falls into the earth and dies, it remains just a single grain; but if it dies, it bears much fruit" (John 12:24). New life from death is both paradoxical and mysterious. Yet, for Christians, this belief constitutes the basic pattern for understanding everything that occurs in life. Christian faith does not deny the reality of pain and death. Instead, it offers images of hope to help us cope with these harsh realities: a crushed grain of wheat bearing rich fruit (John 12:24), the restored life of a Lazarus stepping forth from the tomb after days of waiting on the faithfulness of a friend (John 11:1–44), and a risen Jesus having breakfast with his friends in a lakeside reunion and reconciliation (John 21:9–14). These Christian symbols proclaim that life always prevails over death; there is no need to fear, even when we face the worst that life has to offer. Because God raised Jesus from the dead, we know that reality is ultimately gracious.

For Christians, loss is never the last word. Accordingly, Walter Brueggemann, a noted biblical scholar, provides a map of the spiritual journey that corresponds to the paschal mystery of God's bringing new life from death.[9] According to Brueggemann, spirituality is our walk with God through recurrent patterns of: being securely oriented, being painful disoriented, and being surprisingly reoriented. This pattern repeats itself in all the areas of our lives where we encounter the divine: in relation to the self, others, and the world.

Brueggemann's conceptual map of our earthly sojourn matches our real-life experience. If we reflect on our life history, we can readily recognize the phases he describes. Periods of being securely oriented are marked by a sense of well-being and security: good health, rewarding work, loving family, close friends, and money in the bank. Faith is secure and we feel that God is in God's heaven and all is right with the world. When we are enjoying secure orientation, we wake up singing, "O, what a beautiful morning!"

Yet, we know too well that these moments of security can be quickly shattered. All it takes is the quiet invasion of a microscopic virus to compromise our immune system and lay us low for weeks or a long-distance call that informs us that a loved one has been diagnosed with terminal cancer. Quirky earthquakes and other unpredictable disasters constantly remind us that the phase of painful disorientation can make a sudden entrance, dramatically changing the landscape of our lives.

And because we have survived the many stormy seasons of our lives, we also know from experience that life is fluid. We change; things and circumstances in our lives change. Losses such as death, divorce, illness, or unemployment fashion a free space where new perceptions—like faith, hope, and love—may find hospitality. These sorts of changing life-circumstances "can dismantle the complacent sensibilities we have thus far cultivated and send us seeking. We are stripped bare in the breech. Unmasked in the unfamiliar disequilibrium. In our nakedness we are somehow more vulnerable to the divine touch."[10] Then in mysterious and graceful ways, our struggles abate, our life is resituated, and we are once again surprisingly reoriented after a painful period of disorientation.

- After months or years of grieving the loss of a loved one, the tears finally dry up and a desire to reengage with life emerges.

- The anxiety of a career change precipitated by a layoff gives way to the challenge and excitement of new work.

- Grandchildren are born and their needs reactivate our capacity to nurture life.

Surprising reorientation points to the life-giving presence of the God of Easter in our lives.

Gratitude Reflection: To foster a spirituality of gratitude, it is important to remember our "resurrection moments," i.e., times when we have experience new life from a death-like loss or when an unexpected blow knocked us for a loop, leaving us worried about whether we could keep going. Such reflection not only enhances our gratitude for God's sustaining grace, but also deepens our hope and trust in the reliability of God as we move into the future. The paradigm of the paschal mystery helps us see with grateful eyes how our lives are laced with amazing grace.

- How have you experienced new life from a death?

- Can you recall any personal example that felt like surprising reorientation arising from painful disorientation?

The Exodus

The major revelation of God in the Old Testament is the Exodus event, which revealed God to be a compassionate liberator. Etymologically, the word *exodus* comes from the Latin *ex,* meaning "out of" or "away from," and the Greek *ho hodos,* meaning "the way." Literally, it means "the way out." The story of the Exodus recounts the dramatic intervention of God on behalf of the Israelites trapped in the bondage of slavery in Egypt. Suffering miserably, they groan under the weight of their burden; God takes note of their groaning and then takes action by commissioning Moses to intercede with Pharaoh for their release. Having negotiated successfully with Pharaoh, Moses then leads the Israelites out of captivity, but only after being the instrument of God's deliverance when he parts the waters of the Red Sea and provides the Israelites with a safe passage in their escape from the pursuing Egyptians.

Gratitude Reflection: The Exodus is a story of release from bondage. Seen as a paradigm, the story reminds us that God is committed to doing for us today what God did for the Jewish slaves in the time of Moses. God continues to have compassion on those of us who suffer from any form of bondage and will support us in our efforts to find a "way out" to freedom.

Today, there are many ways we can experience being enslaved or stuck. Some of us are locked in the prison of bitter disappointment, unforgiving resentment, consuming envy, or debilitating self-hatred. The Exodus story reassures us that what God did for the Israelites, God continues to do for people today. Surely, gratitude will swell up in our hearts, when we think of those who have been Moses in our life, helping us out of some of these stuck places. Like the Israelites, we are thankful that we have been similarly liberated.

The wide variety of Twelve-Step groups today points out how common the problem of addiction is. There are meetings for those addicted to alcohol, drugs, food, work, codependency, sex, shopping, gambling, etc. When followers of Twelve-Step spirituality turn their uncontrollable lives over to a Higher Power, they are banking on the reliability of the God of the Exodus to lead them out of enslavement. Viewing their struggles through the lens of the Exodus enables them to have hope for release and gratitude for divine support. "Grateful alcoholics," for example, say at meetings that they are grateful because their addiction with alcohol has not been *in the way* of spiritual growth, but has proven to be *the way* to a deeper and more meaningful life than they might otherwise have had. It is appropriate that the alcohol and drug rehabilitation unit in certain hospitals is called the "exodus unit," since it aims to give addicts a "way out" of enslavement.

- Have there been "stuck places" in your life, from which, through the grace of God, you have been rescued?

- Who has been a Moses for you, when you needed guidance and support?

The Burning Bush

One day while tending his father-in-law's sheep in the desert, Moses happens to notice a bush that is aflame, but not being consumed. Drawn by curiosity, he approaches the bush. Suddenly, however, he hears a voice—the voice of the Creator of the Universe, the Lord of history—say to him: "Moses…come no closer! Remove the sandals from your feet, for the place on which you are standing is holy ground. I am the God of your father, the God of Abraham, the God of Isaac, and the God of Jacob" (Exod 3:4–6). When Moses heard this, he "hid his face, for he was afraid to look at God."

Gratitude Reflection: This biblical story tells of God's surprising appearance to Moses, while engaged in his daily routine. As a scriptural lens, the story can help us claim similar moments when we have felt addressed by the living God. A bush in the desert aptly symbolizes the ordinary. Yet, it is a spiritual truth that with eyes of faith, every bush can be a burning bush, revelatory of God. As a scriptural paradigm, the story of the burning bush attunes us to the ongoing self-disclosure of God in the mundane circumstances of life.

- Have you experienced "burning bush" moments, when you felt God revealing something special to you, something that enabled you to live with more meaning, clarity, joy, freedom? The revelation may have been contained in a commonplace experience, such when reading a novel, hearing a passing comment of a friend, or watching the evening news on television. Remembering these precious epiphanies in ordinary life will enhance your gratitude.

- Moses' encounter with the Holy One was not in a church or sacred place, but in nature. Can you get in touch with moments when you have been enthralled by the beauty of a star-studded sky and felt enveloped by a Love that reassured you that all will be well and that there is nothing to fear? Or when the sun's rays warmed your heart and made you grateful to be alive?

Numinous Dreams

Dreams, sometimes referred to as "God's forgotten language," can serve as conduits to God. We call some dreams "numinous," because somehow they convey God's presence and guidance. As the psalmist states, God gives to the beloved even in sleep! The biblical stories of Joseph (Matt 1:18–25) and the three Magi (Matt 2:1–12) illustrate numinous dreams that reassure the dreamer of God's intimate involvement in their lives. In these two stories, the protagonists are in the midst of some perplexing struggle: Joseph, sleeping fitfully and wrestling with what to do about his engagement to Mary, who, to his bewilderment, is pregnant; and the three kings, vulnerable travelers in a foreign land, searching for clues in their quest of the Christ-child. Joseph is given divine guidance in a dream that instructs him to resolve his conflict by going ahead with his marriage plans. In obedient faith, Joseph accepts Mary as his wife and takes her into his home. And the wise men are warned in a dream not to return by way of King Herod's territory, because the evil intentions of the threatened king put them in harm's way.

Gratitude Reflection: In our clinical practice, we (Noreen as a Jungian analyst and Wilkie as a spiritual director) have had many people tell of a consoling dream that increased their faith, hope, and trust in God. In our personal lives too, each of us has benefited from such dreams, especially when discerning major life choices.

- Can you recall any such dream in your life through which you gratefully received reassurance, direction, and support at a scary time of transition or confusion?

- Sometimes, even when we cannot recall the specific details of a dream, we awake with a lingering sense that God is with us and that in the end all will be well. Can you recall and be grateful for such moments?

Grace Breaks Through Barrenness to New Life

The stories of Sarah, the aged mother of Isaac (Gen 17:15–19), the mother of Samson (Judg 13:2–7), and Elizabeth, the mother of John the Baptist (Luke 1:36–38)—three women thought to be barren—illustrate the creative power of God who gifts us with new life, even when we feel doomed to hopeless sterility. These accounts of God's grace breaking through barrenness may help us to recognize similar situations in our lives, when we were amazed by how new life emerged from what we thought was a barren and useless place.

Gratitude Reflection: The stories of Sarah and Elizabeth evoke much marvel, because these two women were not only barren, but very old in years. When God revealed to Abraham that he would have a son through Sarah, "he laughed, and said to himself, 'Can a child be born to a man who is a hundred years old? Can Sarah, who is ninety years old, bear a child?'" (Gen 17:17). Elizabeth, "who was said to be barren," also conceived a son "in her old age" (Luke 1:36). At a time of increasing longevity, Sarah and Elizabeth can serve as important reminders of the power of God, who can bring about newness even in our senior years, fruitfulness even when old age tempts us to think that our productive years are long over!

- Are there places in your life where you have been surprised by new growth and fruitfulness, after giving up hope that something new and exciting could happen? Perhaps, it was in pursuing a lifelong dream or passion that was put aside because of the demands of earning a living. Taking the risk of pursing this deferred dream in midlife or after retirement has brought about fresh vibrancy to life.

- Are there areas in your life where you find much satisfaction and joy, after long years of dutiful, though difficult, investment without noticeable results?

- Have you experienced the surprise of getting pregnant after many futile attempts? Or discovering that someone close to you is expecting a child, after losing hope that this would happen?

The Visitation

Soon after the Angel Gabriel's announcement that she was to become the mother of the "Son of the Most High," Mary set out to visit her elderly cousin Elizabeth who was six-month pregnant. Upon her arrival, Mary was greeted with surprising, though joyful, news! With a loud cry, Elizabeth said to Mary, "Blessed are you among women, and blessed is the fruit of your womb. And why has this happened to me, that the mother of my Lord comes to me? For as soon as I heard the sound of your greeting, the child in my womb leaped for joy" (Luke 1:42–44). The mystery of the Visitation conveys the good news that the blessings of God often come to us through the hands of family members. In the exchange of care and concern among relatives, through the months and years of familial contact, we often experience the embodied love of God. As was the case with Mary and Elizabeth, the visit of a loved one in a time of need can be a graced encounter.

Gratitude Reflection: Reflecting on the visits of relatives and close friends with the lens of the Visitation can restore appreciation for the love that upholds our lives. Too often we tend to take for granted the love and support of family members and those nearby.

- Can you recall a time when you needed help (e.g., you were ill, recovering from childbirth, or grieving a heart-breaking loss, feeling depressed) and someone visited you?

- Can you recall a conversation with someone that filled you with consolation and deepened your sense of God's faithful presence?

The Parable of the Prodigal Son

Among the better-known parables told by Jesus is the parable of the prodigal son. It is a parable replete with rich images of the good news Jesus came to proclaim. First, the parable likens human life to an unrestricted gift that we receive from the hands of a loving God. With no strings attached, the creator gives us time and energy, talents and opportunities to live a life that is fulfilling for ourselves and others. Like the younger son, we too are allowed the freedom to search out a way of living and working that brings us contentment. Second, the parable communicates the good news that we live in a multiple chance universe and that God allows for trial-and-error learning. Like the prodigal son, we can always expect God to give us another chance, even when our initial exploration lands us in a cul-de-sac. The Good News is that we are allowed to learn through mistakes and if we fail, we can always go home—not to a scolding, but to a celebration set up by a God who is crazy with delight that "this son of mine was lost and is now found, was dead and has come back to life."

Gratitude Reflection: As a scriptural paradigm, the parable of the prodigal son invites us to view our life as an unrestricted gift from God. An African catechism gives a delightful response to the question, "Why did God make us?" In the spirit of this parable, it states, "Why, because God thought we might enjoy it!" Human life is meant to be enjoyed as a gift, not dreaded as some kind of obligation to live out a blue-print determined by God. An added gift is that we are given the freedom to choose and many chances to discover what we want to do with our "one, wild, and precious life."

- How have you experienced forgiveness and a second/third chance?

- Who has been a prodigal parent figure in your life, welcoming you home in your brokenness and affirming your goodness and potential in spite of your past failures?

The Lake Crossings

Multiple gospel passages recount the disciples' crossing of the Lake of Tiberias in the midst of a threatening storm. The lake was known for its unpredictable nature, its capacity to suddenly whirl into a tempestuous and precarious swell. Thus, crossing the lake was always a risk, especially so in the darkness of night. It is typically at night, when Jesus directs the disciples to "cross over to the other side." The phrase "to cross over to the other side" captures the literal meaning of the term "transition," which comes from the Latin *trans*, meaning "across" and *itus*, which is the fourth principal of the Latin "to go." Transitions in life are often scary, because they necessitate leaving a known and familiar place for a new and strange place, but first having to endure the in-between-time of uncertainty. This story aptly illustrates the nature of life transitions. In all of the gospel accounts, however, Jesus appears to the disciples, beginning to panic as the fierce winds and waves mount in intensity. In the midst of their fear, he comforts them with the divine reassurance: "It is I. Do not be afraid." Then, they are brought safely to the other side, once again on solid ground.

Gratitude Reflection: The journey of life is punctuated with multiple transitions: leaving home to live on our own, starting out on a new career after graduation from college, getting married and starting a family, changing jobs to take advantage of opportunities or to stay afloat economically, retiring from work, and finally, confronting the transition from this life to the next. Remembering people who have embodied Jesus' reassuring support for us in times of anxious, perhaps stormy, transitions is a way of enhancing our gratitude.

- Whose names and faces surface to your mind, when you think of people who have helped you through important life transitions?

- From whom have you heard echoes of Jesus' reassurance, when you have faced the difficult transition, occasioned by the death of a spouse or by divorce?

- Who has been a reassuring presence when you were laid off and had to find a new job or undergo retraining to start a new career?

Lens of Forgiveness and Second-Chances

Many gospel stories graphically convey that God's forgiving and merciful love stands as the centerpiece of the Good News proclaimed by Jesus. In Luke's Gospel, a penitent woman who expresses her contrition for past sins by washing Jesus' feet with her tears and wiping them dry with her hair is herself washed with forgiving love and given a second chance (7:36–50). In John's Gospel, a woman caught in adultery and about to be stoned to death, is rescued by a merciful Jesus, who sends her off to start a new life (8:3–11). John also recounts the encounter of Peter with the risen Jesus at the Sea of Tiberias (21:9–19). In this first Easter, Peter received the gifts of reconciliation and re-commission. Perhaps the last time Peter was in Jesus' presence was when he locked eyes with the captured Jesus, whom he had just denied three times in the courtyard of the high priest. If this is true, then it is easy to imagine Peter's gratitude and relief when his relationship with Jesus and his call to be leader of the primitive church, which he had forfeited by his betrayal, were both restored.

Gratitude Reflection: As paradigmatic stories, these Gospel accounts of divine forgiveness are meant to tell us not only what God has done in the past, but what God is always doing.

Gratitude will well up in our hearts, when we spot the similarity between our situation and those of gospel figures who were the beneficiaries of God's forgiving love.

- Who has forgiven you and allowed your relationship to be restored after a betrayal?

- Who has defended you in your attempts to repent and reform your life, after going down a wrong path?

- Who has given you new chances after initial failures?

Jesus' Baptism in the Jordon

Jesus addressed God as "Abba," an Aramaic term that is best translated as "papa" or "daddy, "in order to capture the intimacy that the term connotes. Given his image of God as a loving father, it seems clear that his religious experience when being baptized by his cousin John in the River Jordan was foundational for his life. In that experience, he witnessed the clouds above part and heard God say to him: "You are my beloved in whom I take great delight!"

The struggle for self-esteem is pervasive in our society. For whatever reason, many of us experience an underlying, often unconscious, feeling that we are not good enough to be loved and accepted for who we are. Because of this, we need the healing grace of seeing ourselves as we are in God's eyes: lovable and acceptable. The very sight of us delights God. It is noteworthy that Jesus received his affirming experience of divine favor at the River Jordan *before* the start of his public ministry. This fact highlights the truth that God's love for us, as it was for Jesus, is based on our *being, not on our doing*. Like Jesus, we are the apple of God's eyes. God's love created us and continues to sustain us in existence at every moment. We are the beloved of God, simply because God has chosen us to enjoy that status, not because we in any way have earned it by our personal qualities and achievements.

Gratitude Reflection: Just as Jesus was the Beloved of God, we too as his followers are meant to assume the same identity. Grace strikes us when our goodness and lovableness are mirrored in the eyes of people in our lives. Their loving gaze makes it possible for us to internalize fully the truth of our worth. When we recall who has so mirrored our goodness to us, our hearts are filled with loving gratitude for them.

- Who has concretely embodied the message of God's unconditional love and delight in you? Your mother or father? Your grandmother or grandfather? Your spouse? Your children? Your best friend through the years?

- Who has been a John the Baptist figure in your life, facilitating a peak experience of feeling deeply cherished for being who you are?

The Bent-over Woman (Luke 13:10–13)

While there are many accounts of Jesus' showing compassion to those in need, the bent-over woman cured by Jesus serves as a powerful symbolic lens to help us see with grateful eyes when we have been similarly touched by God. Jesus is teaching in the synagogue on a Sabbath, when he notices out of the corner of his eye "a woman who for eighteen years had been possessed by a spirit that crippled her; she was bent double and quite unable to stand upright." Seeing her, Jesus is moved with compassion and calls her over. He then touches her and says to her: "Woman, you are freed from your disability." At once, the woman straightens up glorifying God and looks straight out on the world, for the first time in a long, long while.

It is not difficult for us to identify with this bent-over woman. We need not be suffering from osteoporosis to do so. The complex challenges and problems of life in our fast-paced society can be so burdensome at times that we too feel weighed down and bent-over. Fortunately, the approach of a compassionate Jesus has come in the form of people who have noticed our suffering and helped to lift our sagging spirit.

Gratitude Reflection: We can imagine that this woman, whose life was so dramatically altered by Jesus' healing touch, was filled with gratitude for this unsolicited act of kindness. To foster gratitude, recall those who have noticed your oppression and have reached out to lighten your load.

- Who has noticed you at a time when you felt weighed down with life's cares and came over to alleviate your burden?

- Who is regularly committed to lifting you up in prayer and thus allowing you not to feel alone and unsupported?

The Wedding Feast at Cana (John 2:1–12):

"The story of Jesus changing over a hundred gallons of water into fine wine at a wedding in the village of Cana," states biblical scholar Marcus Borg, "is regarded by virtually all mainstream scholars as a purely metaphorical narrative, not as a report of a historical event."[11] Nevertheless, the perennial truth wrapped in this story is central to the gospel of John. John features the wedding at Cana as the dramatic opening scene of Jesus' public ministry and uses this inaugural story to say "what the story of Jesus is about, what constitutes the good news." To the early readers of John's account, mention of marriage and a wedding carried important significance. As a rich religious metaphor, marriage evoked the covenant relationship between

God and Israel and between Christ and his bride, the church. Moreover, a wedding feast, in the hard and meager existence of Jewish peasant life at the time of Jesus, was the most festive of celebrations, a momentary release from unremitting hard work and a time to enjoy a time of plenty, filled with food, wine, music, and dancing. Given this context, Borg points out why the opening story of the wedding feast at Cana was a powerful way of conveying the good news: "*the story of Jesus is about a wedding.* And more: it is a wedding at which the wine never runs out. More: it is a wedding at which the best wine is saved for last. All of this flows from a more-than-literal reading, from hearing the story as a metaphorical narrative, from a parabolic reading of it."[12]

Gratitude Reflection: This story of Jesus generates gratitude by proclaiming that the reign of God, inaugurated by Jesus, is meant to bring joy to our often-difficult lives. It tell us that we can celebrate, because there is in our midst a reliable Source of abundant life. A grateful heart is mindful of those in our life who help to transform the water of mundane life into the wine of joyful celebration, as at the wedding feast of Cana.

- Who are people in your life whom you can count on, when celebrating life's joyful moments (like significant birthdays and anniversaries)?

- Whose presence in your life can be counted on to bring surprising joy at moments of disappointment?

"Seeing" God in a Child's Face

This scriptural paradigm enables us to recognize with gratitude how God's loving presence is often reflected in the face of a child. The fragile, yet stunning, beauty of a newborn renews our sense of the miracle of childbirth and of the giftedness of all life. Scripture presents this paradigm in the story of Simeon and Anna (Luke 2:22–38) and the three kings whose search ends in grateful adoration in the manger in Bethlehem (Matt 2:1–12). At the appointed time, Mary and Joseph bring the infant Jesus to the temple in Jerusalem. As they enter the temple, a holy man named Simeon approaches them. Pulling aside the cloth covering the baby's face, he bends close to get a good look at the child. He beams with joy and excitement as he looks long and lovingly into the infant's eyes. He then straightens up and utters a prayer of deep gratitude and praise to God for fulfilling the promise of a savior in the birth of this child.

Just as Simeon ends his prayer, Anna, the eighty-four year old prophetess who spent her days in the Temple serving God, comes by. She too looks long and lovingly at the child Jesus and breaks out in praise because she sees in the face of this baby the messiah promised by God.

Gratitude Reflection: The story of Simeon and Anna invites us to recall moments when we have delighted in the face of an infant, perhaps at the birth of one of our own children or that of a grandchild, niece, or nephew. Dwelling over these moments is a way of fostering gratitude.

- When has the face of an infant brought delight to your eyes, as it did for Simeon and Anna?

- How have you experience God through children? What valuable lessons have children taught you?

Fostering Gratitude through the Prism of Other Gospel Stories

The following are but a small sampling of other scriptural paradigms that can serve to shape our perception in gratitude-enhancing ways.

- Mark and Luke recount how friends had to lower a paralyzed man on a stretcher through a hole in the roof so that he could reach Jesus, who was crowded in by a multitude of people seeking healing (Mark 2:1–12; Luke 5:17–26). Who performs that helping function for you? A close friend, therapist, or spiritual director? Someone who has confronted you in tough love and challenged you to get the help you need for recovery? Or someone who invited you to a prayer meeting, where you had a religious experience?

- John provides a vivid description of Mary Magdalene's encounter with the risen Jesus, as she stood frozen in grief before the empty tomb. Thinking that she was talking to the gardener in her frantic search for the missing body, Mary suddenly recognizes her beloved when she hears a familiar voice lovingly call out her name, "Mary!" (John 20:1–8). Who calls out your name in a similar way that makes you feel deeply loved and accepted, just as you are?

- John recounts how Peter came to meet Jesus only because his brother, Andrew, went to find him to share that he had met the Messiah (John 1:40–42). Who has shared their faith-story with you and helped you to encounter God for yourself? People in your church or faith community? Authors of spiritual books? Singers of "gospel music?"

- Mark recounts that Simon of Cyrene, a passer-by, was enlisted to help Jesus carry his cross (15:21–22). Who helps you bear a cross that burdens your life?

- Recall moments when you, like St. Paul on the road to Damascus (Acts 9:3–9; 22:6–11; 26:12–18), encountered God in a dramatic way, when you felt struck by grace or experienced a sudden shift within that brought joy and gladness.

- Recall times when you encountered grace in quiet moments, like Elijah who experienced God, not in a mighty hurricane or a powerful earthquake or a blazing fire, but in "a small still voice" (1 Kgs 19:9–12).

- Recall surprising events in which you experienced the provident care of God, as Jesus talks about in Matthew 6:25–34 and Luke 12:22–32: "Therefore I tell you, do not worry about your life....And do not keep striving for what you are to eat and what you are to drink...your Father knows that you need them....Do not be afraid, little flock, for it is your Father's good pleasure to give you the kingdom" (Luke 12:22, 29, 32).

NOTICING GRACE WHERE WE LIVE

Prayerfulness consists in noticing the divine presence that permeates life. God is nearer to us than we realize, for it is in God that "we live and move and exist" (Acts 17:28). Grace has been homogenized with the ordinary. An affirming word when failure has devastated our self-confidence, a look of understanding when death of a loved one has rudely ruptured years of companionship, an ice-breaking word of reconciliation that ends a bitter family feud—all point to the inspiring Spirit's presence. Other movements of grace are traceable elsewhere, sharpening our instincts of compassion and love: experienced, for example, when we shed our cautious feelings to reach out to the homeless or when we work against our sexist resistance to female ministers. Situations like these serve as our burning bush, signaling the presence of the living God and enlarging our capacity for gratitude and thanksgiving.

In this chapter, we have suggested some scriptural lenses or paradigms that can train our perception to notice how grace abounds in a world drenched in divinity. Our faith does not cause us to see different things, but to see things differently. By giving us an eye for God, scriptural paradigms remind us that God is more present than we think. We grow in gratefulness as we become more aware of the rich manifestations of God's gracious generosity in daily life.

❧ SPIRITUAL EXERCISES AND REFLECTION ❧

Imaginative Contemplation of Scripture

We have suggested in this chapter how scriptural lenses can enhance grateful living by helping us detect the presence and action of God in ordinary life. Experiment with the prayer-experiences suggested below. Write down in a journal what happened in your prayer and how you were moved. Share these prayer experiences with someone who might benefit from them.

Being God's Beloved

Those of us who experience feelings of inner emptiness, inadequacy, and shame struggle with being grateful. We need the healing grace of seeing ourselves as we are in God's eyes: lovable and acceptable. The very sight of us delights God.

Biblical Passage

The Baptism of Jesus in the Jordan (Mark 1:9–11; Matt 3:13–17; Luke 3:21–22)

Prayer Experience

1. Find a quiet place, where you can be alone and undisturbed for a period of thirty to forty five minutes.

2. Say a brief prayer acknowledging God's presence and ask for the grace to be open to being touched by God.

3. Read the text a couple of times slowly, and take in the event that the text is relating: What is happening and how does the action unfold? Who are the people involved? How do they feel about each other and what is occurring?

4. Put the text away. Now with your imagination, see the dramatic action of the scene unfold, as if you were witnessing the event as an outside observer.

5. Notice especially what Jesus experiences as his cousin, John the Baptist, pours water on his forehead. Imagine Jesus' looking up and seeing the heavens part and then hearing the voice of the Creator of the universe say to him: "You are my beloved in whom I take great delight." As Jesus takes in what is happening to him, imagine his whole body being filled with the warm glow and fullness of God's affirming love.

6. Next, put yourself at the edge of the riverbank and imagine yourself somehow being drawn to John the Baptist to be baptized and to enjoy the same experience that Jesus had. Imagine yourself tentatively dipping your feet into the river and feeling the soft mud at the river's bottom ooze gently through your toes. Then you start to move towards the middle more boldly because you find the water cool and welcoming. Then see yourself standing in line, waiting your turn. Suddenly, you find yourself in front of the Baptist and he starts to pour water on your forehead. At that moment, you look up and see the heavens part and you hear the voice of the Creator of the universe say to *you*: "You are my beloved in whom I take great delight."

When you hear these words, you feel your whole body warm up with the glow of God's affirming love. Remain in that moment and absorb what has just been addressed to you. Allow God's reassuring voice to resonance deeply throughout your being, filling up your inner pockets of emptiness and pain with healing love.

Called by Name

Biblical Passage

The Appearance to Mary of Magdala (John 20:11–18)

Prayer Experience

1. Begin by following steps 1–4 of the prayer-exercise above.

2. With the eyes of your imagination, see Mary outside of the tomb of Jesus, weeping. She peers inside the open tomb and finds Jesus' body missing. Two angels in white sitting where the body of Jesus had been ask her, "Woman, why are you weeping?" "They have taken away my Lord," she replies, "and I do not know where they have laid him." Turning suddenly, she sees Jesus standing there, though she does not recognize him. Jesus says, "Woman, why are you weeping? Whom are you looking for?" Mistaking him for the gardener, Mary answers, "Sir, if you have taken him away, tell me where you have laid him, and I will take him away." Jesus says "Mary!" At that moment, hearing Jesus say her name, she recognizes Jesus and reaches out to him.

3. Now imagine that you are roaming about the garden of your ordinary life, feeling depressed, lonely, and empty. Suddenly you bump into a stranger, who, to

your surprise, calls you by your name. The very moment you hear the loving and endearing way your name is called out, you recognize the Risen Jesus and are filled with consolation.

Comments on the Exercise

Mary of Magdala, like others whose encounter with the Risen Jesus is described in the resurrection narratives, is meant to be a figure or type with whom we are called to identify. Her experience, in other words, is meant also to be ours. Her recognition of the Risen Lord is triggered by her hearing a familiar and loving voice call her name. This account in chapter 20 of John's Gospel is charged with added meaning when we hear it in light of what Jesus said ten chapters before when describing himself as the Good Shepherd:

> I am the good shepherd. I know my own and my own know me… (10:14).

> My sheep hear my voice. I know them, and they follow me (10:27).

In this prayer-exercise, we ask for the grace to recognize the voice of the Risen Jesus calling out our name with warm affirmation and acceptance, just as he spoke Mary's name in the garden. An experience such as this can bring healing to the wound caused by not feeling seen, recognized, and valued for who we uniquely are. Gratefulness will naturally flow from such an experience.

CHAPTER 4

Obstacles to Gratitude

❧

Do not spoil what you have by desiring what you have
not; but remember that what you now have was once
among the things only hoped for.

—Epicurus

SPIRITUALITY SEEN AS A PATHWAY must be concrete to be helpful. As
a guide to the human journey, it cannot simply be a way in the
mind, but must also be a way in the world. In the last two chapters we have elaborated how faith can provide a strong foundation for a spirituality of gratitude. In this chapter, we identify
three obstacles that confront us in developing a spirituality of
gratitude: corrosive envy that eats away at our ability to recognize
and appreciate the good in our lives, narcissistic entitlement
that makes us take our gifts for granted, and a consumerist mentality that touts material possessions as the key to happiness. We
will discuss how each impedes our ability to live gratefully and
how, as a kind of unholy trinity, they feed and abet each other.

ENVY AND GRATITUDE

Whenever we see others enjoy something we that we value,
but lack, envy can enter our heart, disturbing our sense of peace
and filling us with frustration. Envy sows seeds of discontent by
stirring up feelings of sadness and deprivation, even when we

have everything we need. Severe attacks of envy, moreover, cause us to feel anxious, depressed, even resentful and hostile toward those who seem to have more than we do, as if they have taken what should be ours. One of the most powerful human emotions, envy can take us over and transform us into green-eyed monsters, insatiable and greedy for more. All major religions have long recognized what the studies of positive psychologists have recently verified, that envy wrecks havoc in human relationships, pitting people against each other and causing divisions in families, religious denominations, political parties, and nations. Envy is often considered the worst of the seven "deadly sins" because it replaces humility and gratitude to God with entitlement and ingratitude, and in so doing, breaks the tie that connects creature to Creator.

In a consumerist culture that daily exposes us to images of things that are desirable, it is as easy to be infected by envy as it is to catch the flu. Whether we are conscious of feelings of envy or deny it altogether, we cannot escape the long reach of the media with its ongoing reminders of the advantages that many enjoy. We are bombarded with false promises of the happiness and fulfillment that can be ours, if we just purchase whatever product our favorite actor or sports hero is selling. It's easy, just put it on a credit card! In First-World countries the most obvious forms of envy are financial (more money, bigger house, classier car), prestige (fame, power), and appearance (perfect body, latest style, most expensive anything). The calculated, but subliminal, message is, "You are what you have." "Happiness can be bought." "The good life is measured by how much you possess." Before we realize it, we can be caught up in the web of envious comparisons that drive a "healthy" economy and lose touch with our own deeply held spiritual values. We start to feel entitled to things. That life owes us, or people owe us, even that God owes us.

How Envy Erodes Gratitude

Comparing ourselves with others can trigger envy. The story of a middle-aged man illustrates how envious comparisons get stimulated.[1] Happily married to a woman with whom he felt physically and psychologically compatible, he was pleased with his college teaching job and his respectable, if modest, salary. He lived in a good neighborhood and his children benefited from quality public schools. Socially, he was satisfied with friendly colleagues and acquaintances, as well as with several close friends. Overall, he felt quite content about his life—that is, until he attended the twentieth reunion of his college graduating class.

Curiosity about how time and circumstances had treated his former classmates brought him to the event on campus. But curiosity quickly turned into envy when he discovered that many of his classmates had attained greater social, economic, and professional status than he had. Not only did they make more money and had what sounded like more exciting jobs, but their children went to elite private schools and their wives seemed more interesting and attractive than his.

The envious feelings stirred up by his discovery destroyed his contentment, and he returned home from the reunion disgruntled, feeling inferior and like a failure. No longer happy with his spouse, he resented her for not being more like the wives of his classmates. Whereas he was once satisfied with his position as a college professor, he now was dissatisfied with his modest income and the monotony and lack of influence of his job. He harbored a secret animosity towards his successful friends, as well as a barely conscious hope that some setback would befall them. In short, comparing himself with others at the reunion created an onslaught of envy and resulted in ongoing psychic pain that tainted the way he viewed his whole life. In the brief span of a weekend, envy clouded his perception and blinded him to the good in his life that he once enjoyed.

Envy makes it difficult to see one's own God-given gifts and potentials. Envious people focus so intently on what others have, that they become blind to what is their own. They have difficulty identifying and appreciating their own unique gifts, because they always have the feeling that others are more talented than they are. As a result, their gifts are lost to them. The very things that could bring them a sense of satisfaction, self-worth, and accomplishment are hidden in the shadow, that psychic store-house for all the disowned parts of the self. And because whatever is in the shadow gets projected onto others, they see their neglected potentials reflected in the achievements of those around them, and resent them for enjoying what they long for.

A couple of examples can help to illustrate the way in which this happens. A woman attending a faculty party with a friend finds herself feeling miserable as the evening progresses. She notices how relaxed and vivacious her friend is and how others naturally gravitate toward her. In contrast, she sees herself as a wallflower, self-consciously shy and fearful. She wishes that she could be more spontaneous and sometimes she resents her friend for always being the center of attention. She judges her as insensitive and selfish. But deep down, she knows the truth: she is envious and would give anything to be her! The moral of this story is not that the wallflower should try to imitate her extroverted friend, but that she needs to explore the anxieties and fears that keep her from moving out toward others, as she secretly desires.

In other cases of envy, people find themselves obsessing over the material possessions of others. A self-made business-man, for example, is envious of his neighbor, who owns a larger business and a new Mercedes. He feels inferior to his neighbor, whose wealth and power exceed his own. That he is a successful husband and father now seems unimportant to him, because he believes that a man's worth is measured by money and prestige. Because of the symbolic importance he has placed on these things in recent years, he has lost his appreciation of the family life that was once his first priority and source of happiness. That which formerly provided a sense of fulfillment and pride no longer satisfies him. Envy has robbed him of the riches that he once treasured.

The Roots of Envy

Envy drives some people to do their best, motivating them to pursue their goals and go after what they desire, while in others it activates painfully recurrent feelings of deprivation that immobilize them. We do not know exactly why some people can turn envy into something positive and others are defeated by it, but this question has long been a topic of interest for psychologists and sociologists. Most notable among these is psychoanalyst Melanie Klein (1957) who views the conflict between envy and gratitude as inherent in human nature. She suggests that a predisposition or propensity to envy is rooted in infancy when a child is totally dependent on its mother. If, for whatever reason, adequate nurturing is unavailable, the child despairs of ever getting what it needs. These early experiences of maternal deprivation cause feelings of abandonment and damage the child's ability to depend on others. Later in adulthood, she believes, this early failure in the mother-child relationship can manifest itself in a proneness to envy and ingratitude.

In contrast to the psychoanalytic position, social theorists believe that envy is the by-product of living in a "culture of envy." Envy, they suggest, is the engine that drives today's institutions—schools, businesses, government, media, and the family. The bumper sticker, "The one who dies with the most toys, wins," is a stark expression of how our culture has enshrined the competition to acquire more things as its dominant value. "Our educational system teaches skills for external success," states one social theorist, and "Our modern media forms prodigious, mesmerizing machinery geared toward disseminating envy-inducing images." This creates a culture of envy, because "In response we squander our souls by chasing an ever-widening array of things we do not need. But no one has it all, leaving all to envy those who have more. So the economic forces of modern culture conspire to promote the envy on which it is based."[2] Naturally, those who are predisposed to envy due to childhood deprivation are more susceptible to such cultural inducements.

It can be argued that the tendency to compare and compete is, to varying degrees, in all of us. We often judge ourselves and others on the basis of achievements, such as academic success, financial prosperity, a happy childhood, a great social life, prestigious job, attractive luxuries, and so on. When the painful absence of some good makes us envious, we can respond in one of two ways. The envious feelings can motivate us to pursue long forgotten or postponed goals, and in so doing our envy is redirected and gainfully employed in the service of our own enrichment. Or our envious comparisons can take us down a more destructive path and diminish our self-worth, causing us to either withdraw from life ("It's no use!") or driving us compulsively to pursue one goal after another in a futile attempt to boost our fragile self-esteem. Whatever our life circumstances happen to be, it is important that we take notice of how we respond to the envious feelings that can sneak up on us at any given time. Whether we are blessed with abundance or struggle just to make it, we can decide to count our blessings and be grateful for what we have, or we can count other people's blessings and feel cheated. Developing a spirituality of gratitude in our contemporary culture of envy and narcissistic entitlement is truly countercultural; it challenges us to maintain a balance between our human propensity to always desire more and our soul's need to gratefully embrace that which makes us all equal, the gift of life itself.

A Spiritual View of Envy

Envy is the result of not appreciating the depths of desire that our human nature experiences. To be human is to have pockets of emptiness that endlessly hunger for fulfillment. St. Augustine's prayer, "You have made us for yourself, O God, and our hearts will remain restless until they rest in You," expresses the truth about our deep yearning, a yearning that leaves us feeling forever incomplete and pining for more. It is precisely this infinite dimension of our desires that keeps us longing for fulfillment. When we do not consciously embrace this aspect of our human condition, we become frustrated and envious. We forget that we are creatures destined to find completeness only in divine love. Envy makes us think, "if only I had such and such, I would finally feel complete." But eventually, as experience repeatedly bears out, disillusionment sets in and we come to devalue the very thing we thought would satisfy us. Instead of accepting limitation and loss as part of life, envy turns us into victims who think that others always have more and that no one ever gives to us. Feeling like victims, we hold others responsible for what is missing in our lives. We blame them and want revenge, as if they should pay for our unhappiness. What begins as our own suffering gradually becomes something that someone else has done to us. The emptiness and longing that we once felt are replaced by resentment and rage. And those who possess what we desire become the enemy, whose happiness is at our expense.

While it is important to understand the psychological and cultural dimensions of envy, confronting this obstacle to gratitude requires that we clearly see how envy undermines us spiritually. Faith tells us that God has uniquely fashioned each of us, right down to the number of hairs on our heads. Further, we have been created in the image of God, suggesting that God had an image of each of us "before we were knitted in our mother's womb," a unique, never to be duplicated image. As a radical refusal to accept our being in all its uniqueness, envy is both a rejection of self and a rejection of God because we cannot reject the gift without rejecting the Giver. Theologian Johannes Metz contends, "Self-acceptance is the basis of the Christian creed. Assent to God starts with [our] own sincere assent to [ourselves], just as sinful flight from God starts with [our] own flight from [ourselves]."[3] Satan is the archetypal envier because he could not accept himself. That he was not God was intolerable to him, so he rejected God, creating a kingdom of his own wherein he could reign. Milton makes this point in *Paradise Lost*, where he declares that envious rebellion entered the world through Satan:

> The infernal serpent; he it was, whose guile,
> Stirr'd up with envy and revenge, deceived
> The mother of mankind (book 1, line 34).

Faith also teaches us that as Christians we are meant to be always in longing until that day when God becomes our all in the heavenly Jerusalem. A spirituality of gratitude invites us to see the poverty that we experience as creatures, not as a negative void to be lamented, but as a rich vacancy for God, who alone can satisfy our being.

Since gratitude and envy are mutually exclusive, the way to heal an envious heart is to replace it with a grateful heart. This is one of the purposes of prayer: to remind us of the gracious generosity of God and to awaken in us a sense of appreciation for the goodness that is already ours. Prayer moves us deeply into the mystery of grace. In prayer, we open ourselves to the abundance of God; here our emptiness becomes a gift, rather than a curse, as God fills us with love. The more desperate we feel, the more we know our need for God. And in humility we begin to recognize the gifts and graces bestowed on us over our lifetime. Occasionally, when we least expect it, a grace we have long needed comes to us, and like C. S. Lewis, we are surprised by joy. Even our sufferings and losses become occasions of grace as we realize we were not abandoned, even when we abandoned ourselves. When gratitude becomes our way of life, we make peace with our envy, not excusing it or ignoring it, but acknowledging it as part of ourselves. Then, with the psalmist, we can pray: "It was you who created my inmost self, and put me together in my mother's womb; for all these mysteries I thank you: for the wonder of myself, for the wonder of your works" (Ps 139:13–14).

NARCISSISTIC ENTITLEMENT

"Entitlement" is an attitude of expecting something without having to do anything in return. One of the greatest obstacles to developing a spirituality of gratitude is an internalized sense of entitlement. Ours is a culture that nurtures the narcissistic belief that "I" come first and that "life owes me." When we feel entitled, our rights come first, before everything and everyone else. If we think that something is owed to us and we don't get it, we feel cheated or, if we do get it, we deserved it! It is important here, however, to distinguish between a healthy sense of entitlement and what we are calling narcissistic entitlement. People cognizant of their self-worth know that as human beings they are entitled to be treated with respect and dignity. The American Declaration of Independence proclaims that we possess certain inalienable rights, chief among them the right to "life, liberty, and the pursuit of happiness." People who have a robust sense of self-worth expect to be treated with fairness and respect, but they are also able to accept that this does not always happen. They feel grateful when things go their way, but are not undone by disappointment or inequity. In contrast, narcissistic people are self-centered, ungrateful, and unforgiving; it's all about them, their rights, what they've got coming to them. An attitude of narcissistic entitlement undermines gratitude and replaces it with ingratitude. "Why should I be thankful for this, since I've got it coming to me? I'm owed it!" When we receive something that we regard as ours by rights, we feel gratified, but not grateful.

Narcissists: Born or Bred?

Psychologists believe that narcissism is an inherent stage in child development and a normal phase in establishing a healthy sense of identity. When we use the term "narcissistic" to describe adult behavior we are referring to a syndrome that is caused by a failure to outgrow that early self-centered "me" stage.[4] A narcissistic person is someone who has a grandiose sense of self-importance and entitlement, an excessive need for admiration, and lacks empathy for others. Narcissistic personalities "expect to be given whatever they want or feel they need, no matter what it might mean to others."[5] What causes people to be narcissistic is debatable, but various researchers have suggested the following possible factors: an oversensitive temperament at birth; parental overindulgence; excessive admiration that is never balanced with realistic feedback; unpredictable or unreliable care giving from parents; severe emotional abuse; excessive praise for good behaviors or excessive criticism for poor behaviors. Freudian theorists are more specific about the childhood etiology of narcissism. They believe there is a crucial window in development between ages three and seven, when children need recognition and approval of their talents and gifts. This experience of "being seen" is so crucial to healthy ego development that its absence sentences the child to a lifelong struggle with feelings of inferiority, often masked by feelings of entitlement, and an inability to tolerate life's inevitable frustrations and disappointments.

Cultural Manifestations of Narcissistic Entitlement

Society as a whole has moved increasingly toward becoming a culture of entitlement. In a review of the sagas of several infamous CEOs, a *New York Times* article concludes that narcissism is epidemic in corporate America and suggests that narcissistic entitlement may, in fact, be an occupational hazard in the business world.[6] In contrast to psychiatrists who believe that narcissism has its roots in early life, business management researchers suggest that adults can learn to be narcissists, if they are in a system that encourages such behavior. Narcissism, they say, is a part of the human condition and it tends to flourish in the absence of checks and balances. Most top-level executives do not set out to act unethically or criminally, but they can be carried away by the adulation and power bestowed on them. A kind of "romance of leadership" puts top executives on a pedestal, observes a professor at the London Business School and "[t]his can become a liability if the leaders begin to believe they are geniuses."[7] He cites the Enron executives as a classic example. "They begin to believe they and their organizations are one-of-a-kind, that they're changing the face of industry. They desire entitlements beyond any other C.E.O.'s."[8] Analyzing the narcissistic personality in the financial world, Sam Vaknin comments, "The narcissist regards himself as one would an expensive present. He is a gift to his company, to his family, to his neighbors, to his colleagues, to his country."[9] The narcissistic executive's inflated sense of importance "makes him feel immune to mortal laws and somehow divinely protected and insulated from the inevitable consequences of his deeds and misdeeds."[10] One might conclude that the culture of entitlement that has thrived over recent years bears a share of responsibility for the gradual unraveling of some of our best industries.

There are close parallels in the world of politics. Political psychologist Stanley Renshon finds that "Narcissism is an occupational hazard for political leaders. You have to have an out-sized ambition and an outsized ego to run for office."[11] Or as one disgraced politician put it, "You begin to think of yourself as master of your own universe and your own set of ethical structures, your own sense of decision-making."[12] Psychologist Frank Farley has extensively studied the behavior and personalities of politicians and coined the term— "Type T personality." The "T" stands for thrill-seeker, a trait that he suggests is built into their personalities. "Politics has very high levels of uncertainty, variety, novelty, challenge, unpredictability and therefore attracts a certain kind of person."[13] Political scientist Fred Greenstein uses the concept of adrenaline rush to describe the common denominator in the personalities of politicians. They have a strong need for excitement and in this kind of life there is an abundance of temptation. He agrees with others that narcissism is also a clue to the personalities of politicians.

> These are men who love themselves deeply, need to be recognized and relish approval. These are men who adore getting praise and who often are surrounded by swarms of sycophants. These are men who, in some cases, need to exercise power and sometimes can become drunk from it. These are men who think the rules don't apply to them and who think they're untouchable. As leaders, these are also the type of men who are likely to break promises, manipulate and cut corners. They probably are big risk-takers. And they're prone to thinking of themselves first.[14]

While the ordinary person has a difficult time understanding this, one political strategist, when asked about this propensity for politicians to take potentially career ending risks, was philosophical in his response, "As long as we keep electing people to public office, we're going to keep getting flawed people. One of my favorite songs about this kind of thing is 'The Most Unoriginal Sin.' That's what this is. It's not that complicated."[15]

CONSUMERISM FUELS PERPETUAL DISSATISFACTION

The "consumerist culture is a prescription for permanent suffering," asserts *Los Angeles Times* columnist Joel Stein, in a satirical piece called "The Key to iHappiness." He provides an amusing illustration of how a consumerist mentality managed to undermine his gratitude by fostering discontent, when an electronic upgrade, like the iPhone, surfaced as the latest must-have "in thing." Stein writes:

> The shame began Jan. 11 when Steve Jobs unveiled the iPhone.
>
> I was inundated with reports about the world's totally perfect gadget that, when I had to check my messages at dinner that night, I cupped my hands around my phone to hide it. I was convinced that everyone in the restaurant had an iPhone, and they were using it to play some kind of new Brazilian dance hall mash-up they had heard about in iPhone texts from their new supermodel friends, all the while sliding caviar into their mouths off the perfectly smooth iPhone whose glowing screens bathed their faces in soft light like a Caravaggio painting.
>
> My Treo—which until that morning seemed like a gift from eager-to-please aliens from the future—humiliated me. And shame is not something I feel easily....
>
> It wasn't until I looked out at the sea of Blackberries that I remembered the iPhone wasn't coming out for

almost six months, which made me feel a little better. But not much.[16]

Stein's experience mirrors what many of us feel and aptly describes what feeds our need, if not compulsion, to consume. Manufacturers fuel our discontent with a strategy of planned obsolescence and continual upgrades for existing equipment. Inner voices of insecurity and inadequate self-worth are amplified by advertisers whose livelihood depends on creating and expanding "needs." Advertisements aim to convince us that what we have is not enough and that happiness is just one more purchase away. As Stein humorously confesses, "I know, for a fact, that if I can just have an iPhone, I will be completely happy forever. I will be really careful and never drop it and charge it every night and use it only for very important things—like texting everyone I know messages such as 'I have an iPhone!' "[17]

Understanding some of the psychological and cultural underpinnings of consumerism can help us curb its course. At its core, consumerism's magical spell over us relies on the hopes and expectations we place on consumer products. Name brands and designer labels, for instance, are purchased with the hope that they will increase our self-esteem and raise our social status. With the candor of a satirist, Stein shares more of his self-talk as he deals with the shame evoked by not owing an iPhone.

> The saddest part is that when the iPhone comes out at 6 p.m. next Friday, I won't buy one....I want people to know I'm the smart guy who waits for Apple to fix the bugs, lower the price, make it thinner, increase battery life, add three gigs, offer more service providers and install a retina scan that prevents people my age from going on MySpace.
>
> But even though I know better, my tech-lust will rage. I will walk up to iPhone-sporting strangers, like a

pigeon to a bus driver, and beg them to let me use theirs. None of that lust will come from any genuine desire to listen to music on the same machine I use to make phone calls. Unless I move to New York or Tokyo or actually go running, I don't need my music with me at all times....

My jealousy will stem from the simple fact that an iPhone makes a person both important and cool. The iPhone Dude is a guy who might, at any second, get a key work e-mail, send a photo of his date to friends...and he doesn't have time to pull out a bunch of different gadgets. Which means that his time is more valuable than Batman's.[18]

Like Stein, many of us are susceptible to the enticements of greater personal importance through what we own. "As a guy," Stein admits, "gadgets are the only tools we have for expressing our importance. Women have jewelry, clothes and social lives. We've got cars, phones, large TV screens and women."[19]

Advertisers promise that their products will fill the voids in our lives, satisfying not only our physical needs but also our emotional longings. The latest fashions promise to make us attractive and appealing, thus playing on our unmet need to be loved. These subliminal messages are so effective that "many couples concentrate on owning a house or filling it with nice furnishings, when what they really crave is an emotional construction— home."[20] In a consumer society, material goods are also called upon to serve as reassurances of love and care, as when absent parents attempt to assuage their children's feelings of abandonment–and their own guilt—by indulging them with every imaginable toy or game. The psychology behind promotion and advertising is so effective that intelligent, rational adults will go into debt, spending up to the limit on several credit cards at a time, so that they can fulfill their loved ones' every material desire. Unfortunately, everyone pays the price for this kind of overspending—those who must overwork to keep creditors at bay, and their loved ones who feel cheated and bereft of a spouse or parent who is never at home.

Stein's satirical critique of the pursuit of happiness based on an unbridled consumerist approach to life exposes how consumerism undermines gratitude by fueling discontent. His conclusion resonates well with a spirituality of gratitude:

> So I'm going to hold off as long as I can before buying an iPhone. I'm going to learn that the only way to be happy is to understand that I have everything I need, and I need nothing I don't have. That the consumerist culture is a prescription for permanent suffering. That my bulky, lumbering Treo with its tiny screen, cluttered buttons, limited Web browsing and pathetic "Pocket Tunes" is just fine.
>
> But it's definitely time I get a flat-screen TV.[21]

Chronic Dissatisfaction Impedes Gratitude

Joel Stein's depiction of how we can become captives of consumer goods is easily identifiable in ourselves and in others. That it is a widespread occurrence is understandable when we see how it is culturally induced. Ingratitude, it seems, is ingrained into our worldview and economic system, which relies on perpetual dissatisfaction to expand consumption. "Consumerism works only as long as we are even slightly dissatisfied with what we have," states Mary Jo Leddy in her *Radical Gratitude*, an analysis of how a consumerist culture erodes grateful living. "Perpetual dissatisfaction," contends Leddy, "is integral to an economic system, that expands to the extent that it can continue to expand the needs and wants of consumers. This artificially induced craving becomes a habit of being, perpetual dissatisfaction."[22] A pithy recap of her argument goes like this:

> We cast our eyes around the things we have bought at great price, at the experiences we have accumulated and the relationships we have acquired and find them all somehow...wanting.
>
> This dissatisfaction is not natural. It is a culturally induced dissatisfaction that is essential to the dynamic of the culture of money....We are enticed by the promise that with just a little bit more of whatever we would be happy and satisfied....We are held captive by dissatisfaction.[23]

The *Simpsons* nicely illustrates the ungrateful mentality that a culture of money can create. Saying grace before a meal, Bart prays, "Dear God, everything we are about to partake in, we paid for with our own hard-earned money. So thanks for nothing!" While comical, the attitude expressed here is, nevertheless, common. As Leddy points out:

> In the culture of money, we tend to have a ledger view of life. We add up the pluses and the minuses and try to account for our lives. In the process, we miss the amazing fact that we even have a life to add up. We take being alive for granted and move on to a cost-benefit analysis. Lost in the process is the incalculable mystery of simply being alive. The liberation of gratitude begins when we stop taking life for granted.[24]

A spirituality of gratitude must seriously consider this argument, if it is to recognize realistically the huge challenge entailed in living with satisfaction in an environment that breeds discontentment. This spirituality must foster a return to the simple joys of life. As Leddy puts it, "Radical gratitude begins when we stop taking life for granted. It arises in the astonishment at the miracle of creation and of our own creation."[25] Only when such a renewed appreciation for our blessings is regained will the vicious cycle of dissatisfaction with life be broken. In gratitude, we can then "begin anew in the recognition of what we have rather than in what we don't, in the acknowledgement of what we are rather than in the awareness of who we aren't."[26] Gratitude is an attitude that enables us to appreciate that we have everything we need for today. Worry about tomorrow's needs undermines gratitude and expresses a lack of hope in God who knows our needs even before we do.

Struggling with Good Enough

Addressing the issue of a "culturally induced dissatisfaction," Leddy states that "[t]he craving for more is inversely experienced as the sense that what we have is *never enough*" (emphasis in the original).[27] She cites the example of billionaire Howard Hughes. When asked how much money it would take to make him happy, he reportedly replied "just a little bit more." While Hughes has been depicted by his biographers as being somewhat eccentric, it was clearly not his assumption that more money is the secret to happiness that made him stand out as odd! In this, his thinking resembled a common belief and made him like so many of us. "In the culture of money, Leddy remarks, "we begin to believe that if we just had a little bit more of whatever we would be happy but what we have now is not enough. The objects of our craving may change, but the dissatisfaction will remain."[28]

Positive psychologists have investigated the question, "If we are so rich, why aren't we happy?" This question naturally arises when we consider why people do not seem to be getting any happier in the midst of our culture of increasing abundance. In fact, some have argued that the increasing rate of depression and suicide suggests that the misery index is increasing even as material prosperity has abounded—in spite of economic cycles. Psychologist Philip C. Watkins, in discussing the relationship between money and happiness, reports, "research has shown that happiness can't be bought."[29] A reason given by psychologists to explain why happiness is not inevitably enhanced by increases in material blessings is related to the "principle of adaptation." Researchers from several different areas in psychology have found that we have an amazing ability to adapt to our changing circumstances. From the context of emotion theory, this is referred to as the "law of habituation." According to this law, we tend, over time, to get used to our current level of satisfaction. This habituation then leads to taking things for granted, lessening our appreciation and gratitude in the process, for "the realities we take for granted can no longer be recognized as an amazing grace, can rarely astonish us into life, will never set us free."[30] Take, for example, a professional athlete who may be unhappy or perhaps feeling somewhat deprived, despite his $500,000 annual contract, because his salary has remained the same for the last five years, and others on the team are making more. In this example, we see two obstacles to gratitude combined: the tendency, over time, to get used to our material blessings, and our proneness to feel less appreciative of what we have because others have more. As Leddy wisely reminds us, "Our general dissatisfaction with ourselves, with others, and with the world is possible only as taking for granted becomes a habit of being. We can want more because we assume we already have something or someone."[31]

Consumer Goods Cannot Provide Lasting Satisfaction

As helpful as psychology can be in explaining why money and material possessions often fail to provide us with the happiness we long for, we must turn to our Christian tradition to discover the roots of our dissatisfaction. Christian spirituality asserts that deep within the human heart is a hunger and longing for God. The psalmist gives eloquent expression to this desire:

> As a deer longs for flowing streams,
>   so my soul longs for you, O God.
> My soul thirsts for God,
>   for the living God.
> When shall I come and behold
>   the face of God? (Ps 42:1–2)

> O God, you are my God, I seek you;
>   my soul thirsts for you,
> my flesh faints for you,
>   as in a dry and weary land where there is no
>   water.…
> Because your steadfast love is better than life,
>   my lips will praise you (Ps 63:1–3).

Lasting happiness comes only in satisfying this hunger. Sometimes we experience our hunger for God in the pure form of an intense desire for union with the divine. Other times, however, our hunger for God is intertwined with a myriad of human longings:

- in a longing to be deeply understood and unconditionally accepted for who we are, just as we are;

- in an abiding feeling of homesickness that reminds us that our hearts yearn for a place beyond our earthly existence, a heavenly Jerusalem, where there will be no longer any sadness or tears;

- in an ongoing, seemingly relentless, search for intimate relationships that can dissolve all loneliness.

Because our hunger for God wears the guise of some of these other human longings, it can often be missed or not understood for what it truly is. Thus, we can feed the wrong hunger when we try to wring from material goods the happiness and satisfaction that can only come from the transcendent Creator of those goods. In short, we must distinguish between "psychologically based dissatisfaction and the deeper existential dissatisfaction that is one side of the mysterious longing for God."[32]

In our pursuit of happiness, many of us unwittingly set ourselves up for frustration. We imagine that we are "essentially a passive receptacle, a self whose happiness consists in being filled 'to the brim.'"[33] This image leads to endless disappointment because we eventually discover that when it comes to satisfying our desires, we are more like a bottomless pit than simply a receptacle of needs. It's not surprising, then, to read about millionaire athletes and superstars who have the financial resources "to have it all" committing suicide or dying from drug overdoses because they despair of ever finding happiness. Christian spirituality offers us a truer understanding of the self and the nature of human fulfillment. Rather than a passive receptacle or collection of desires to be fulfilled, the self is "a dynamic spring, a self that is realized only in its active movement beyond itself"[34] to a love of God that finds its concrete expression in the loving service of others.

At age seventy-five and after a lifetime of pursuing the spiritual path, Jungian analyst Robert Johnson writes in his memoirs,

> Most of our neuroses come from hunger for the divine, a hunger that too often we try to fill in the wrong way. We drink alcohol, take drugs, or seek momentary highs through the accumulation of material possessions. All the manipulations of the outer world carry with them

an unconscious hope of redeeming our lonely, iso-
lated existence.[35]

Just as we feed the wrong hunger when we compulsively overeat
to fill up an emotional emptiness, in a similar way we can place
unrealistic demands on consumer goods to satisfy the deepest
hunger of our heart, which far outstrips the capacity of anything created to satisfy. Echoing this truth, theologian Wendy
Farley states, "A consumer culture is an oversized example of
the misery brought about by an effort to still desire with possessions....The dissatisfaction of desire arises from desire itself; it
cannot be satisfied with any finite thing or even an infinite number of finite things, and can be destructive."[36] St. Ignatius of
Loyola's prayer, the *Suscipe* ("Take, Lord, and Receive"), captures
beautifully the Christian wisdom that reminds us that only
God's love can ultimately liberate us from our perpetual dissatisfaction and provide us with a sense of "good enough." Thus,
he taught us to pray, "You have given all to me. To you, Lord, I
return it. Everything is yours; do with it what you will. *That's
enough for me.*[37] Through grace, Ignatius grasped fully the truth
that when we have God, we have everything. And there is nothing more than everything.

SPIRITUAL EXERCISES AND REFLECTIONS

A Reflection Question on Envy

Recall times when you felt pleased when you heard of
another's misfortune, or when you secretly rejoiced in another
person's failure. Can you recognize how these were moments
when you were experiencing envy? At each of these times, at
whom and about what were you envious?

A Reflective Exercise to Expand Gratitude and Generosity and to Check for Narcissistic Entitlement[38]

Complete the following sentence stems:

- What have I received from others (list specific people/gifts)? _____

  _____

- What have I given to others (be specific)? _____

  _____

  _____

- What trouble and difficulties have I caused others (be specific)? _____

  _____

This exercise incorporates a Buddhist mindfulness technique called *Naikan*. Used as a psychotherapeutic device in Japan to help people develop balance in their interpersonal relationships, it can help us monitor (a) to whom and for what we need to be thankful (first question); (b) how we have given to others or been generous (second question); and (c) how we may, by our thoughts, words, and actions, caused unhappiness or disharmony in our relationships.

The second and third questions relate directly to the obstacles to gratitude discussed in this chapter. Question two can alert us to any sense of entitlement that makes us content to always being on the receiving end but never on the giving end. To stay vital, relationships need to be reciprocal; each person must give, as well as receive. Narcissistic entitlement impedes gratitude; genuine gratitude naturally fuels generosity.

Question three's relevance to fostering gratitude will become more apparent in the next chapter, which addresses healing and forgiveness as a way of clearing the pathway to gratitude. Briefly stated, forgiving others for a deep hurt or wound they might have caused us is made easier when we can acknowledge our own weakness and brokenness.

This practice of asking these three questions can be done daily, especially if we are experiencing trouble in a significant relationship, or periodically to help us monitor the quality of gratitude and generosity in our interpersonal life.

De-cluttering Our Consumerist Hearts

St. Augustine once said that God is always trying to give good things to us, but our hands are full of things to which we are inordinately attached. And not only our hands, but our hearts and minds are cluttered with objects of attachment that distract us from God.

1. What fills your life to the extent that God is crowded out?
2. How can you make "awareness space" for God in your life?

Healing the Deprived Inner Child through an Experience of Being Seen

Biblical Passage

The Presentation of Jesus in the Temple (Luke 2:22–38)

Imaginative Contemplation Experience

1. Begin by following steps 1–4 of the first prayer exercise, "Being the Beloved," at the end of chapter three.

2. With the eyes of your imagination, see Joseph and Mary with the infant Jesus in her arms climbing the steep steps of the Temple in Jerusalem. As they enter the section of the Temple where the child is to be presented to God, a holy man named Simeon approaches them. Moving aside the cloth covering the baby's face, he bends close to get a good look at the child. Notice how he beams with joy and excitement as he looks long and lovingly into the infant's eyes. He then straightens up and, with a heart bursting with gratitude and praise, he prays:

Master, now you are dismissing your servant in peace,
   according to your word;

for my eyes have seen your salvation,
   which you have prepared in the presence of
   all peoples,

a light for revelation to the Gentiles
   and for glory to your people Israel.

3. Just as Simeon finishes praying, Anna, the eighty-four-year-old prophetess who spent her days in the Temple serving God with fasting and prayer, comes by. She too looks long and lovingly at the child Jesus and breaks out in praise because she sees in the face of this baby the promised Messiah, sent by God to establish the Kingdom of God.

4. Notice how the infant Jesus is so alert and attentive to both Simeon and Anna as they hover over him with admiration and love. Their warm smiles, gentle touch, and adoring eyes fill Jesus with a deep sense of being special and loved.

5. Now imagine that you are the infant in Mary's arms. Joseph is there, as are Simeon and Anna. They draw gently near to you and, by turn, ask to hold you. As you are passed from one person to the next, you see your own lovableness and specialness reflected in the eyes of these adults who bend over you with such obvious affection and appreciation. Imagine how their affirming reactions fill your being with a deep sense of your goodness.

Comments on the Exercise

An underlying, often unconscious, feeling that we are not good enough to be loved and accepted for who we are frequently contributes to compensatory behaviors that end up in frustration and thereby diminish our gratitude for our life. In order to gain love and win approval, we become addicted to helping others and making ourselves indispensable. This deficit in self-esteem often stems from childhood experiences of emotional deprivation. The theme of the inner child or the "child within" has been developed by such theorists as W. Hugh Missildine, MD, and Eric Berne, MD, to describe a conscious, consistent pattern of thoughts, feelings, attitudes, and behaviors that resemble or re-create the experience a person had as an actual child. The term is popularly used in such self-help groups as Adult Children of Alcoholics (ACA) to help people better understand their sense of emotional deprivation and emptiness, stemming from childhood experiences of neglect, abuse, or abandonment in dysfunctional families.[39]

As children, we need to receive confirming responses from the significant others in our lives regarding our specialness and lovableness. This explains why children often want to be the center of attention, actively seek the praise of others for their accomplishments, and yearn to be the apple of their parents' eyes. When our parents or primary caregivers do not mirror our specialness in a way that satisfies this need, our ability to feel lovable and attractive is gravely impaired. Psychologists refer to this impairment as a "narcissistic wound." Imaginative prayer, such as the above exercise, can contribute to the healing of the deep hurt that results from not having received adequate mirroring in childhood.

CHAPTER 5

Clearing the Way to
Grateful Living

❦

In this life, happiness is rooted in our basic attitude
toward reality.

—THOMAS KEATING, OCSO[1]

AT MEETINGS OF ALCOHOLICS ANONYMOUS, people frequently conclude an account of their painful struggles with a clear statement
of gratitude: "I'm so grateful!" To those who are unfamiliar with
Twelve-Step spirituality, this is truly perplexing! How, we ask ourselves, can they be grateful for the pain and suffering brought
about by their addictions? Why are they not feeling frustration,
anger, and hurt that they have had to encounter so many obstacles in their life? Experienced addiction counselor and pastoral
theologian Patricia Nanoff explains what makes recovering alcoholics grateful, when she shares, "The answer lies in the shift in
attitude that takes place in recovery....No one has a barrier-free
life. In recovery we learn to appreciate the very obstacles that
used to frustrate us and rob us of our serenity."[2]

   This appreciation stems from a trusting faith that with God's
enabling grace what once stood as roadblocks on our journey can
be turned into pathways of possibilities. Gratitude wells in the
hearts of "grateful alcoholics" for the simple fact that they are
alive and can tell their story, whereas once their out-of-control

drinking could have, at any time, caused death and devastation. In the language of biblical spirituality, this basic attitudinal change is called *metanoia,* literally meaning in Greek, a transformation in the way we perceive and respond to life. It contains the core wisdom of Twelve-Step spirituality. It is a genuine conversion of heart.

What is true for "grateful alcoholics" is true for all of us. As Thomas Keating wisely states, "In this life, happiness is rooted in our basic attitude toward reality." Contentment with life deepens to the extent that we view our lives with gratitude. Thus, a spirituality of gratitude fosters an ongoing conversion of heart that moves us from feeling entitled to everything we have to feeling grateful for the gift-nature of everything, from needing to control everything in our life to a peaceful acceptance of our reality, even when it does not conform to our desires. The well-known Serenity Prayer provides wise guidance by encouraging us to take responsible care of our lives where we have some control and then to hand the rest over to God's care. We are invited to pray: "God, give me the serenity to accept what I cannot change, the courage to change what I can, and the wisdom to know the difference."

The path to grateful living is not as smooth as the popular literature on gratitude sometimes seems to suggest. Child psychotherapist Susan Dyke points to some of the complex and often-unconscious barriers to living with gratitude, when discussing the resistance she encounters among the troubled youth in her practice. While referring specifically to her young clients, her comments suggest what prevents some of us, even in adulthood, from feeling and expressing our gratitude. Commenting on her work with an adolescent girl, whose phobias during puberty resulted in an almost total retreat from normal adolescent life, Dyke illustrates how struggles with forgiveness and gratitude kept her young patient from getting better. At a point in the treatment, when obvious improvement was being made, her patient refused to acknowledge her progress. The young woman told her "that *if* she was getting better, and she didn't say that she was, but *if* she was, then she certainly wouldn't tell me," explained Dyke, "because then I would think that I had done it and she didn't want me to have that pleasure!" This protestation gave Dyke an insight into the meaning of her client's resistance to getting better. Not acknowledging the good that was taking place was her way of withholding any pleasure or joy her parents might feel. "Such was her anger and envy of her parents that she couldn't allow this," Dyke explains. "They, like me, were not to feel they were able to be really fruitful, she would punish them and me by being an unrewarding baby/patient." Generalizing from this case, Dyke makes the point that unconscious rage can prevent people from improving, because getting better implies forgiving those who have hurt us.[3]

"Getting better" further implies gratitude, which "necessitates an acceptance of vulnerability and neediness." Being dependent can be intolerable for children who, feeling abandoned by their parents or primary caregivers, now expect all adults to be equally unreliable. Their resistance to getting better protects them against "the potentially terrifying state of dependence [that] has to be accepted before the gratitude, the feeling of having received something good from outside themselves, can be felt."[4] These therapeutic observations provide the backdrop for this chapter, in which we discuss three interrelated hurdles to gratitude: preoccupation with regrets, clinging to resentments, and reluctance to confront painful emotions in a way that can lead to healing.

REGRETS AND GRATEFUL LIVING

Regret, like a nagging voice of complaint, is an obstacle to grateful living, when it distracts us from living fully in the present. Passing regrets are part of everyone's experience and, truth be told, some things in our lives *should* be regretted. Being human, each of us can regretfully recall times when our words or actions caused pain and suffering. Not to feel regret for these hurtful deeds is, at best, a sign of immaturity and, at worst, a defect in character. Sociopaths, for example, because they have no conscience, feel no remorse. Regret can play a positive role in our lives, if it moves us to repent and keeps us from repeating our mistakes.

Awareness of regrets provides us with opportunities to acknowledge both how we have missed the mark in loving and to make amends for our past shortcomings. In his *A 12-Step Approach to the Spiritual Exercises of St. Ignatius,* Jesuit priest Jim Harbaugh highlights why the Spiritual Exercises and Twelve-Step spirituality encourage us to look at our past regrets. "During the First Week of the Exercises, Ignatius urges us to consider our past, not in a spirit of 'worry, remorse or morbid reflection,' but in light of chances for service" and the healing of relationships. According to Harbaugh, "A clear view of the past is essential if we are going to behave differently now; we can't regret the clarity that leads to healed relationships."[5] When recovering alcoholics put the lessons gleaned from painful experience into service, the "past is alchemically transmuted into a treasure for other people." This is true, not only for recovering alcoholics, but for all of us. When we see how our experience can benefit others, our suffering becomes fruitful and redemptive.

However, regrets become an impediment to gratitude when we get bogged down by "relatively long-lasting and exaggerated regrets," or when regrets begin to dominate our consciousness and "thus assume something like the status of a character trait."[6] John Edgar Widerman's *Brothers and Keepers* provides a helpful illustration of how regret can loom so large in a person's life that it "hangs over one's consciousness like a cloud or mires one's gait like a slough of despond." One of the characters in his book reflects:

> We have come too far to turn back now. Too far, too long, too much at stake. We got a sniff of the big time and if we didn't take our shot wouldn't be nobody to blame but ourselves. And that's heavy. You might live another day, you might live another hundred years but long as you live you have to carry that idea round in your head. You had your shot but you didn't take it. You punked out. Now how a person spozed to live with something like that grinning in his face every day? You hear old people crying the blues about how they could have been this or done that if they only had the chance. How you gon pass that by? Better to die than have to look at yourself every day and say, Yeah. I blew it. Yeah, I let it get away.[7]

Struggling with Regrets

Lingering regrets about decisions and choices that we cannot un-do are like dark clouds that cast a shadow over our life, diminishing our ability to see the blessings of the present moment. The danger of being weighed down by regrets is especially strong in our middle years, when aging and thoughts of mortality prompt us to review our past and assess our prospects for the remainder of life. As we look over our life, we each have our own personal list of regrets for "roads we never took, relationships we never dared, jobs in which we failed, mistakes and follies and accidents and genuine lack of opportunity...[memories of] which return along with feelings of envy or rage or disappointment."[8] At such moments of self-recrimination, we are also swamped with "what ifs." A discontented spirit complains, "If only...I had been born at another time, in another place, I had been thinner, fatter, taller, shorter, cleverer, more sociable, my parents had been different, I had worked harder at school, I had married a different man/woman...and so on."[9] Left unchecked, a discontented spirit can squelch all gratitude from us. Grateful acceptance only comes when we make peace with life on life's terms.

Living Contentedly in a World of Limits

Matter imposes limitations on all of nature, our bodies included. Our experience shows us that all materials things eventually rust, fade, and lose their original form due to wear and tear over time and exposure to the elements. While we tend to deny this unpleasant fact when we are in the bloom of youth, at midlife we are forced to deal with life's built-in limitations, as we come face-to-face with our experience of physical diminishment, career and work disappointments, and unfulfilled dreams for our spouse, our children, and even for our very self. Physically, we experience such things as hair loss, encroaching wrinkles, less flexibility and stamina, thicker bodies due to lower metabolism, diminished eyesight and hearing, and for women, menopause, which signals the end of the childbearing years. At work, we see the writing on the wall warning us that our career is no longer on the rise, but on the decline or stuck on a plateau. We are forced to admit that we have gone as far as we are going when the position we hoped for goes to someone younger, or we must retire sooner than we had planned due to downsizing. In our personal lives, there comes a point at which we realize that some of our earlier dreams are not going to come true and we must struggle to accept our reality as "good enough." We must make peace with the fact that "our spouse is never going to be all we might want. Perhaps most difficult of all, we begin to realize that no matter how hard we work, we cannot always make life come out the way we want it to. In spite of our best efforts, tragic and terrible things happen to people we love and to ourselves."[10] An important challenge at midlife and beyond, therefore, entails humbly acknowledging our limits, while simultaneously striving to live creatively and gratefully.

Coming to grips with our limits as humans is spiritually fruitful, because when we discover our limits, we become more open to encountering "the grace of community and the grace of God."[11] Some of us may have to struggle harder than others to quiet a rebellious part that rails against any limits to our living. Yet for all of us, limits, when accepted with serenity, can expand our capacity to appreciate life and to grow in our relationship with God. In making choices, our "yes" to someone or something often requires a simultaneous "no" to someone or something else. Because we have a limited amount of time, energy, and resources, we must choose among competing goods and desires. Refusal to close the door on certain options can stymie our ability to cultivate an intimate relationship or develop a specialized skill. Holding out on a commitment to marry *x*, with his or her limitations, in the hopes of finding the ideal *y*, who will be perfect, can only result in frustration and despair. In a world of limits, we make choices that necessarily preclude other possibilities. This is the nature of reality. Accepting this fact minimizes regrets for "what could have been" and invites us to deepen our appreciation for "what is."

In their work with the elderly, two Gestalt therapists comment on the debilitating effects of regrets in late life.

> Regrets about choices in life (e.g. choosing a career over children, singleness over marriage, the wrong profession; or a missed opportunity for advancement or failing to express affection to loved ones) can lead to intense feelings of remorse, resentment and depression. Obsessive self-criticism for making what now

seems like a wrong choice often leads to these distressing emotions.[12]

Helping older adults move beyond demoralizing regrets can clear the way for more grateful living. Gratitude, in turn, directly contributes to emotional well-being, as the studies of positive psychologist Philip C. Watkins have shown. His research suggests "that gratitude has a causal influence on mood, especially positive mood." Thus, he argues "the cultivation of grateful emotions might be efficacious in the treatment and prevention of depressed affect."[13] It is important to recognize that both regrets and gratitude can significantly impact our happiness: the more gratitude we experience, the less we tend to dwell on past regrets; the more we dwell on past regrets, the less likely we are to experience gratitude for our life.

Living in the Present with Attention and Awareness

Living wholeheartedly in the present enables us to make the best of our life situation, even in precarious moments, as the following Buddhist parable delightfully portrays. Once there was a man who decided to take a walk through the jungle near his home. As he walked, he suddenly realized that there was a tiger chasing after him. He sped up and came to the edge of a cliff. Fortunately, he spotted a vine that he used to climb down the face of the cliff. Midway on his descent, he looked up and noticed two mice, one black and one white, chewing on the vine. Then he looked down and noticed that there was a tiger prowling down below. Instead of being caught up with self-recrimination about his earlier decision to go for a walk and rather than dreading the precarious future awaiting him, he stayed in the "here and now" and spied a strawberry growing on the side of the mountain. Plucking the fruit, he put it in his mouth and savored it. "Ah," he said, "how deliciously sweet this is."

The point of this parable is clear. Preoccupation with regrets about the past and fretful ruminations about future difficulties can prevent us from enjoying what is before our very eyes! To live life gratefully entails two things: First, not getting lost in the past with regrets, guilt, or nostalgia. For many of us, there comes a time, when serenity will come to us only if we forgive ourselves for our past failures, missed opportunities, and poor choices. Second, not living in the future and feeding catastrophic expectations of what might happen. This means avoiding the trap of "what-if" thinking. Being obsessed with all the possible things that could go wrong is crazy making and paralyzing. Living with appreciation and gratitude requires that we dwell in the "here and now" with awareness of all that the present situation offers.

Awareness Can Reduce Future Regrets

Dwelling on past regrets can contribute to vibrant living, when it helps us identify what we still yearn for in life. It also stirs up gratitude, when we realize that we still enjoy the time and health needed to satisfy these longings. Thus, awareness of regrets expands our freedom by increasing our "response-ability," i.e., our ability to respond in satisfying ways to what we still desire in life. Clarity about our desires can motivate us to do something about fulfilling them and thereby prevent future regrets. In writing about "overcoming the terror of death," psychiatrist Irvin Yalom asks, if we are going to die, then why and how should we live? To avoid the depressing realization of an unlived life at the time of death, he points to a value of regret. "Properly used, regret is a tool that can help you take actions to prevent its further accumulation," he states.[14] If we turn our gaze toward past regrets only to sink into sadness, then reflecting on regrets militates against grateful living. However, if we turn our gaze to the future, suggests Yalom, we "experience the possibility of either amassing more regret or living relatively free of it." This is why he counsels himself and his patients "to imagine one year or five years ahead and think of the new regrets that will have piled up in that period. Then I pose a question that has real therapeutic crunch: 'How can you live now without building new regrets? What do you have to change in your life?' "[15]

Regrets in the Light of Faith

Christians are encouraged to accept the regrets and disappointments of life with a lively trust in the loving Providence of God, who cares for the birds of the air and the lilies of the field and who is totally committed to our well-being. In the end, contentment in life relies on a belief that God desires what is best for us and that God can be trusted. Regrets arise when things do not go the way we planned, when our hopes and desires are dashed. In the midst of these regrets, faith reminds us that God's ways are not always our ways. Sarah and Elizabeth—two women who gave birth to sons when they were long past childbearing age—are biblical reminders of God's mysterious ways. Because God raised Jesus from the dead and brought new life from death, Christian faith reassures us that God can always be trusted and that reality is ultimately gracious. Trusting in the faithfulness of God is central to the message of Jesus. "God always throws a better party" is a colloquial way of expressing this core belief. Thus, we find St. Paul encouraging the community in Rome by reminding them that God works with us in all of our strivings and all things will work together for good (Rom 8:28–29), or as Julian of Norwich puts it, "In the end, all will be well."

A Talmudic story about a certain Rabbi Akiba illustrates well how Yahweh has a way of wringing good out of bad situations and how we must trust in the mysterious and unfathomable ways of God.

In the turbulent first century, the rabbi once traveled in a strange country where mystery still dwelt. He had taken with him three possessions—an ass, a rooster, and a lamp—and had stopped at night in a village where he hoped to find lodging. When the people there drove him out, he was forced to spend the night in a forest nearby. But Rabbi Akiba bore all pains with ease, being heard always to say, "All that God does is done well." So, he found a tree under which to stop, lit his lamp, and prepared to study Torah briefly before going to sleep. But a fierce wind suddenly blew out the flame, leaving him with no choice but to rest. Later that night wild animals came through and chased away his rooster. Still later, thieves passed by and took his ass. Yet in each case, Rabbi Akiba simply responded by saying, "All that God does is done well."

The next morning he returned to the village where he had stopped the night before, only to learn that enemy soldiers had come by in the night, killing everyone in their beds. Had he been permitted to stay there, he would have died. He learned also that the raiding army had traveled through the same part of the forest where he had slept. If they had seen the light of his lamp, if the rooster had crowed, or if the ass had brayed, again he would have been killed. And how did Rabbi Akiba respond? He simply replied as he always did, "All that God does is done well."[16]

Trust in God's loving care for us does not remove the need for responsible striving on our part to live full and vibrant lives. However, it does caution us not to fall into the trap of bitter resentment and ingratitude, when faced with disappointments and regrets.

RESENTMENT HINDERS GRATITUDE

Like recurrent regrets that flood our consciousness and dampen our ability to delight in our gifts, lingering resentments can also impede grateful living. In his study of the life-blessing properties of gratitude, philosopher Robert C. Roberts examines "how gratitude partially dispels, mitigates, or substitutes for" such painful and miserable emotional states such as resentment, regret, and envy.[17] In other words, gratitude and resentment are simultaneously incompatible because as emotions, they tend to exclude one another. According to him, it seems unlikely that we would appreciate the good things that others contribute to our life, strongly sensitive to their good intentions, quite willing to feel indebted to others—*and* at the same time be intensely on the lookout for harm done to us, ever ready to attribute malevolence and neglect to others, and inclined to bear grudges against those who harm us, even in small ways.[18]

If one of the benefits of gratitude is that it prevents resentments from spoiling our happiness, the reverse is also true, i.e. resentments greatly diminish our ability to experience gratitude and other life-giving emotions. *Alcoholics Anonymous,* commonly referred to as the "Big Book" in Twelve-Step spirituality, pinpoints resentment as a major obstacle to living spiritually and gratefully.

> It is plain that a life which includes deep resentment leads only to futility and unhappiness. To the precise extent that we permit these, do we squander the hours that might have been worth while. But with the alcoholic, whose hope is the maintenance and growth of a spiritual experience, this business of resentment is infinitely grave. We found that it is fatal. For when harboring such feelings we shut ourselves off from the sunlight of the Spirit.[19]

Because harboring resentments truly cuts us off from the "sunlight of the Spirit" and grateful living, we turn now to explore the spiritual process of releasing our resentments and restoring right relationships through forgiveness.

Resentment is old anger—suppressed or unattended anger that smolders within like a psychic volcano, dormant yet eruptible at any time. Anger easily turns into resentment when it is neglected, for whatever reason. Some of us "don't do anger," because it does not fit into our ideal of what a good Christian or a "nice" person should be. Or we have experienced the painful devastation caused by the unbridled anger of a "rageaholic" parent or spouse. Others of us fear the potent force of our feelings, and are unsure of how to deal with anger in a healthy way. Whatever the case, no good can come from unattended anger, because anger denied results in depression, guilt, and fatigue, and anger unrestrained leads to hatred and violence.

Anger, which in itself is neither good nor bad, is an appropriate emotional response to injustice, injury, and harm inflicted on us and those we love. The injury we experience can be either physical or psychological. Anger may be warranted at times, when, for example, we suffer unfairness and abuse at the hands of some uncaring party. In such cases, feeling angry is a normal and healthy human reaction. The capacity for anger enables us to avoid being victimized and thus is needed to fuel the protest required by a healthy self-love. Feeling angry in certain situations does not make us resentful persons. It is possible for us to be angry about some things while grateful for others. Being able to feel both at appropriate times enables us to function well as mature persons. However, if we neglect to face our anger honestly, resentment will build up, and eventually it will breed bitterness and undermine gratitude.

What we do with our anger determines whether anger is a constructive or destructive emotion. On the level of experience and awareness, psychological health requires us to be open to our feelings of anger, without imposing any kind of restriction. Restraint and control should come into play only when considering how to express our anger. It is only by allowing ourselves to feel and pay attention to our feelings that we can decide intelligently what to do with them. Repressing anger increases the possibility that we will handle it poorly and eventually "act it out." The critical issue is how best to express our anger, or whether it is desirable to express it at all. When we are able to process our feelings and make conscious choices about how best to handle them, our emotional lives remain vibrant and fluid. If, however, we repress our anger and relegate it to our psychic garbage can, it eventually turns into smoldering resentment.

Human Vulnerability and the Roots of Anger

Vulnerability is a fact of human life. None of us—no matter how much money, power, and prestige we might enjoy—can control all the variables that affect our survival and well-being. Even the wealthiest among us cannot ward off a devastating disaster caused by an earthquake or hurricane. The most powerful among us cannot keep a deadly virus or cancerous cells from ravaging our bodies or those of our loved ones. Such realities as terminal or chronic diseases and accidental or natural calamities ignore socio-economic status and force us all to acknowledge our common vulnerability as humans. In our universe, where randomness coexists with order, accidents, mistakes, and chance account for a good deal of human misery. The bumper sticker, "S*** happens!" reminds us that to be human is to be vulnerable. The resentments that most of us feel, however, flow not from an angry response to acts of nature or random accidents, but rather from hurts, disappointments, slights and betrayals that we experience at the hands of people—family members, friends, teachers, coworkers, and bosses.

Because our existence as humans is precarious, each of us has to deal with a certain "ontological" anxiety. The word *ontological* comes from the Greek *ontos,* which means "being." Anxiety is "ontological," when it refers to the vulnerability that is an inescapable part of the human condition. Out of an innate self-concern and desire to support those we love, it is natural for each of us to discover and pursue a "life project," i.e., a way of "making it" in the world that wards off ontological anxiety. Thus, we set out in adulthood to find ways of accumulating money and possessions, reputation and status, power and control—all the things that, in our minds, will keep us safe and help us contain our anxiety. Given this common quest for security, anger can be seen as a protest against the danger we feel when someone or something threatens our power, self-sufficiency, and personal significance. Power makes us feel in control, able to influence the people and events that affect us. Self-sufficiency alleviates feelings of helplessness and dependence on others, who may end up being unreliable or incompetent. Personal significance grounds our self-worth and communicates to others that our rights better not be violated. Thus, anger is often a response to feeling that others are trying to control us, diminish our worth, or render us subservient or indebted to them.

As we attempt to secure our safety and well-being, we will inevitably have painful clashes with those whose plans and desires collide with ours. Such interpersonal conflicts may evoke anger. However, they need not, if we can realize that most people, motivated by self-concern, are only doing what they think will secure their own well-being. They are not intentionally trying to oppose us. Writing on the process of forgiveness, Lewis Smedes states the importance of differentiating between "suffering sheer pain and suffering painful wrongs." "Not everybody is out to get us. Our lives are cluttered with people who wound our feelings in small ways, but who mean no real harm. We suffer some inevitable aches simply because we are vulnerable people living in a crazy world where fragile spirits sometimes accidently collide."[20] Anger flares up in us, however, when our actions are thwarted by other people's selfishness, greed, and insensitivity. We feel angry when somebody hurts us unfairly, when we are hurtfully wronged by those we trusted to treat us right.

Resentment Resulting from Unfair Pain

The resentments that impede gratitude may be deep-seated and rooted in experiences of abandonment and betrayal of trust. As we negotiate our way through day-to-day life, the chances are that we occasionally experience annoyances, slights, and disappointments, and react to these with momentary flashes of anger, but rarely does this anger turn into deep resentment. When, however, we experience disloyalty or betrayal by those close to us, we can feel deeply hurt and, at times, respond with fierce resentment and hate. "Hatred" is a strong word and most of us have a difficult time admitting our hatred, but "hate," states Smedes "is our natural response to any deep and unfair pain. Hate is our instinctive backlash against anyone who wounds us wrongly."[21] This hate can either be passive, whereby we become indifferent to another's well-being, or aggressive, whereby we become consumed with wishing a person ill. In either case, "Hate eventually needs healing. Passive or aggressive, hate is a malignancy; it is dangerous—deadly, if allowed to run its course," Smedes warns. "Nothing good comes from a hate that has a person in its sights; and it surely hurts the hater more than it hurts the hated."[22]

RELEASING RESENTMENT THROUGH FORGIVENESS

Resentments that smack of hatred are serious obstacles to living a grateful life. Because bottled-up resentment is antithetical to an attitude of gratitude, a spirituality of gratitude must address ways of dealing with resentment that will lead to its release, preventing it from plaguing our lives like a poisonous cloud. "…[W]hen we hate people who do us wrong, our hate stays alive long after the wrong they did is dead and gone, the way the ashen smell of charred lumber lingers with a burned building long after the fire is out."[23] Hate haunts us and deadens our life, blocking out joy and gratefulness. Smedes describes well the dynamics of debilitating resentment and hate.

> We attach our feelings to the moment when were hurt, endowing it with immortality. And we let it assault us every time it comes to mind. It travels with us, sleeps with us, hovers over us while we make love, and broods over us while we die. Our hate does not even have the decency to die when those we hate die—for it is a parasite sucking *our* blood, not theirs.[24]

If we do not seek healing for our wounds, the hate and resentment they cause will forever remain serious impediments to grateful living.

Forgiveness: A Path to Healing

The path to healing ourselves from past wounds begins with identifying and owning our feelings of hatred and pain. It is crucial, Smedes counsels, to distinguish between anger and hate. Anger is a natural and healthy human reaction to feeling hurt or abused in some way. It means that we are alive and responsive. Hate is a sickness in need of healing. Because many of us are embarrassed by our feelings of hate and are unable to feel the depths of our own pain, we deny our hatred, often blaming ourselves as well as others. Hatred that is denied, suppressed, or hidden ultimately becomes a prison, "a hell behind insulated masks of warm conviviality. Hate, admitted and felt, compels us to make a decision about the healing miracle of forgiving."[25] Underscoring the importance of choosing forgiveness over hate, Smedes concludes, "If you cannot free people from their wrongs and see them as the needy people they are, you enslave yourself to your own painful past, and by fastening yourself to the past, you let your hate become your future. You can reverse your future only by releasing other people from their pasts."[26]

Personal suffering can energize and motivate us to work toward changing whatever it is that makes us resentful. We know from experience that deep-seated resentments not only ruin our peace of mind, but also darkly taint our outlook on life, robbing us of the ability to feel the happiness and pleasure that others enjoy. Forgiveness, which comes with releasing resentment, is logically a key component of mental health and happiness. Indeed, psychological research verifies that "a lack of deeply held resentment" is "an implicit component of positive mental health."[27] Unresolved interpersonal problems give rise to lingering resentments and ongoing pain. "A long-standing conflict with a sibling, a child, or a close friend," for example, "remains like an unplucked thorn in one's finger; it can be overlooked and even forgotten at times, but its soreness does not disappear."[28] Forgiveness, by putting closure to unfinished emotional business, sets us free to live more fully in the present and to enjoy the gifts of the moment. A spiritual writer's personal story illustrates the liberating impact of forgiveness:

> I generally try not to hold grudges. But I did nurse one for many years. I had a falling out with someone very close to me. We worked together, we socialized, we made each other laugh. I still remember what caused the rift. It broke my heart. Although we traveled in the same circles, I rarely saw this person any-

more. If our paths did cross, the room suddenly got cooler.

Years passed and I learned that her daughter died suddenly and tragically. I went to the funeral. As I approached, she said, "I need a friend now more than ever." We hugged. It was as if I was released from a trap. I felt the anger and resentment drain out of me.

I wish I knew why I held on to it for so long. I can't think of one good thing it did for me....[29]

Confrontation: When Forgiveness Engages Both Parties

Anger and hurt are an inevitable part of every relationship. The closer and more valued the relationship, the greater the likelihood that we will, at times, hurt each other. When this happens, it is important for the sake of the relationship that we air our feelings and talk about any conflict or tension that exists between us before it can fester and grow. Some of us hesitate to confront others when we are hurt or angry, because we fear that we won't "do it right," or that we will be told that we are "too sensitive." We may even judge such feelings as petty and suppress them, hoping they will go away. But unexpressed feelings do not go away: they build up steam, like a pot simmering on the back burner, until one day they boil over into rage and destructive confrontation. Constructive confrontation keeps us from harboring negative feelings and nursing hurts until they become resentments waiting to erupt. The desired outcome of confrontation is a deeper mutual understanding and a rekindling of a valued relationship.

Contrary to the negative way in which it frequently is viewed, it is important to understand the valuable function that confrontation serves in maintaining relationships. A common stereotype of confrontation associates it with "blowing up," an indiscriminate dumping of pent-up anger and frustration that may help a person unload burdensome feelings, but often harms the ones who bear the brunt of the explosive or hostile personal attack. If we have experienced something like this—at the hands of a parent or a teacher who resorted to verbal abuse as a way of punishing us or of venting their personal frustration, or at the hands of a rageaholic boss or spouse—we will naturally shy away from the very idea of confrontation in our personal and professional lives.

Properly used, confrontation has a twofold function: to invite self-examination and to bridge a distance that has been created. When we confront a person, we are sharing with them not only our feelings (hurt, anger, rejection, etc.), but also describing the particular behavior that upset us, and finally, how we would like to be treated in the future. And because confrontation involves dialogue, we are inviting them to share their perception of the tension between us. Our goal here is to clear the air, and in so doing, to prepare the way for reconciliation. Sometimes this process goes quickly. The other person acknowledges their behavior, understands what we feel and why, and expresses regret. Forgiveness is easy in this scenario, and we move on with our relationship restored. At other times, however, two people can have different perceptions of what happened. If this is the case, we both must take a second look at ourselves. Perhaps we misjudged the other's motives or misinterpreted what they said. Maybe in the back and forth of our honest and open dialogue, one of us becomes aware of something that has been unconsciously affecting our relationship and we both gain new insight. Processing our feelings together in this way can eventually clear the air, dissipate our negative feelings, and restore harmony. It goes without saying, however, that confrontation does not always bring about the desired result. Some people are so defensive that they are unable to look at their behavior honestly and accept responsibility for their actions. If a person can never admit to being wrong or has a million excuses for their poor behavior, our only choice is to keep a safe and self-protective distance and find a way to work through our painful feelings on our own.

Although confrontation can be an effective means of restoring closeness in an important relationship, there are times when it is unadvisable to try it. The persons we confront must care and love us enough to tolerate hearing negative feedback in a non-defensive way, stepping out of their own perceptual framework long enough to genuinely appreciate our point of view. They must value the relationship over their self-image. If safeguarding their pride and righteousness is first and foremost (i.e. they need always to be right), there is little chance that our confrontation will be appreciated or taken seriously. We set ourselves up for more hurt and abuse, if we attempt a confrontation that we can predict will not bring about the result we hope.

Forgiveness When Confrontation Is Not Possible

There are times when the process of forgiving another person must be a kind of personal soul work that we do within ourselves, often with the helpful support of a spiritual director or therapist. When confrontation is not possible because the one who has offended us is unwilling to honestly talk about it (the self-righteous perfectionist mentioned above), or has died (a deceased father who was sexually abusive), or is unknown (a hit-and-run driver or the mother who gave us up for adoption), we can choose to practice a kind of "spiritual surgery" that aims to repair the wrong that was done to us and move us through our anger and resentment to a place of inner peace. Not unlike the method of active imagination used by both Ignatius of Loyola and Carl Jung, this kind of soul work is an effective way of dealing with one's inner world that can bring about healing and forgiveness. "Forgiveness is an *honest* release even though it is done invisibly, within the forgiver's heart. It is honest because it happens along with honest judgment, honest pain, and honest hate."[30]

How do you perform "spiritual surgery" when this is the only option open to you? First, you invite the person who hurt you into your awareness; but instead of remembering them in the familiar way you always do, this time you try to see them "fresh, as if a piece of history between you has been rewritten, its grip on your memory broken. Reverse the seemingly irreversible flow of pain within you." When we do this "The first gift we get is a new *insight.*"[31] Second, this new insight will produce *new feelings.* The new insight has to do with seeing a deeper truth, a truth about this person that our hate blinded us to, "a truth we can see only when we separate them from what they did to us."[32] The gift of this insight enables us to see beyond our hatred and pain to the realization that those who hurt us are human, mere mortals just like us—weak, needy, and fallible. While "our hate wants to cloak them, top to bottom, only in the rags of their rotten deed,"[33] an enabling grace allows us a forgiving look, and we see beneath the tattered rags the truth of their own weakness, brokenness, and fragility. When we forgive we often have to be "content with the editing" of our memory in this way. Graceful healing flows from such editing of our memories because it creates a space for new feelings and a willingness to forgive. "Forgiveness, then, is a new vision and a new feeling that is given to the person who forgives."[34]

While we cannot separate the wrongdoer from the wrong, we can "release the person within our *memory* of the wrong."[35] Forgiving is not the same as absolving someone of responsibility, but the willingness to forgive, without the score being settled, brings healing to our wounded souls. The result of hard and earnest effort, our willingness to forgive is part of what may be a long process of healing. We have come to this place slowly after a long struggle with the desire for revenge and retribution. We have come with the realization that the emotional closure that has eluded us relies not on getting even, but on forgiving. Finally, the new insight accompanied by new feelings offers fresh hope for release from past hurts and resentments. This hope sustains our ongoing efforts until one day we come to the realization that we cannot do this on our own. We need God's grace, if we are to be fully healed.

Admitting Powerlessness: Letting God

Often a confusing ambivalence about letting go of the resentment and hatred caused by past hurts seems to get stronger. Having lived so long with rage and resentment, adults who were sexually abused or felt abandoned as children, for example, have mixed feelings about forgiving their offender. One part of them wants to be finally set free from the burdensome weight of bitter pain, but another part may feel attached to those fiery feelings, despite their debilitating effects. Such feelings have, after all, been part of them for so long that they wonder, and perhaps even fear, how they will have to change if those familiar feelings are gone. A personal experience shared by a spiritual writer illustrates both this type of ambivalence and the power of God's grace to help us let go.

> I woke one morning with a powerful impulse to attend Mass as well as an equally strong desire to go back to sleep. Even more than the extra sleep, I wanted to avoid someone I suspected might attend that liturgy. In the end I obeyed the inner nudge and went to Mass, where I immediately encountered the person I had successfully dodged for years.
>
> I cannot put into words what happened that morning. How do you explain the mystery of forgiveness and reconciliation? I can say that finally letting go of

the familiar feelings of anger, resentment and bitterness was extraordinarily freeing. When I learned that
the person was moving out of state the next morning,
I could only marvel at God's timing.[36]

Twelve-Step spirituality teaches that self-help alone cannot heal us
from the hatred and resentment caused by past wounds; the grace
of God is needed. In fact, only when we acknowledge this need
and surrender our lives to God (or however we understand our
Higher Power) in trustful dependence can liberation and healing
be ours. Our pride and ego may coax us to strain on for years, relying on the multiplicity of self-help tools available to us. Then, by
God's grace, a moment of truth may dawn on us, enabling us to
finally admit our inability to do it on our own. Such seems to have
been the experience of St. Paul, when he cried out in helpless des-
peration, "I do not understand my own actions. For I do not do
what I want, but I do the very thing I hate…I can will what is right,
but I cannot do it. For I do not do the good I want, but the evil I
do not want is what I do" (Rom 7:15, 18–19). As with Paul, only
when we actually *experience* our helplessness can we acknowledge
our powerlessness and need for God. Our utter despair in our
own ability to rid ourselves of painful feelings that chain us to past
wounds may seem at first to be a crisis, but it is in fact a graced
moment that enables us to finally let God be God for us. Renewed
hope comes when we place our trust in the power of God, "whose
power at work in us is able to accomplish abundantly far more
than we can ask or imagine" (Eph 3:20). The miracle of healing
occurs when grace abets our efforts, leading us out of the bondage
of slavery to our past into the promised land of renewed joy and
gratitude for life. If we attempt to sidestep the painful process of
forgiving by forgetting, or if we rush to forgive prematurely so as
not to feel our pain, the result will be a pseudo-solution. Only by
"working the steps" of forgiveness can we be healed. Once we have
truly forgiven those who have harmed us, we can at last forget!

❧ SPIRITUAL EXERCISES AND REFLECTIONS ❧

A Reflection Guide to Healing and Forgiveness

The following reflections are taken from a meditation composed by Herb Kaighan, a recovering alcoholic, spiritual director, and author. Because he has distilled the rich wisdom of the Twelve-Step movement so succinctly and helpfully, we have adapted his meditation into a process guide for dealing with hurts, resentments, and forgiveness. This guide describes the different phases of the healing process and is not meant to be followed in any strict order or time frame. Its usage will depend on individuals and how they find the aspects of the meditation helpful, given their personal background and concrete circumstances.

Facing and Naming the Hurt: Open your mind, memories and heart to remember the hurts, the wounds; recall where and when you have been let down, dishonored, abused, lied to, cheated on, diminished spiritually, emotionally, physically or financially.

Let a picture of the person who harmed you or caused you deep pain freely surface in your memory and mind—your father or mother, husband or wife, boyfriend or girlfriend, brother or sister, relative or friend. If you have been betrayed or hurt by your school, church, the judicial system, the healthcare system, the government, allow the picture of a concrete person who symbolizes the institution surface in your memory or mind.

This is the reality—it did happen—we have been betrayed, hurt, and wounded. Name it and accept it. It is tragic and it is true.

What Forgiveness Entails: It is also true that we can be healed from these wounds.

- To forgive is not to condone or excuse the behavior. What was done was wrong.

- To forgive is not to pardon or exonerate—that's not ours to give—we don't have the power to absolve.

- To forgive is not to forget. We are saddened by the memory and must grieve.

- To forgive is to release from debt; to release from the demand for retribution or retaliation.

- To forgive is to surrender the right to get even. The reality is that as long as we hold on to these hurts, they possess us and poison us emotionally and spiritually.

- To forgive is to take responsibility for our part, which may only be that we have been holding on to these memories and feelings, allowing them to continue to devastate our emotional and spiritual life.

- How long are we going to carry these wounds?

- How long are we going to be shackled by the chain that tows this garbage of hurt, resentment and shame?

Acknowledging Our Own Brokenness: Look at our own brokenness—the pain and hurts for which we have been responsible.

Look at our motives and role in the events in which we find ourselves suffering unfairness, disloyalty, or betrayal. Where were we selfish, dishonest, angry, or afraid?

Acknowledging the Brokenness of Others: In light of our own brokenness, look at *their* brokenness. See how they are like us. Those who have hurt us are themselves hurt, fearful, wounded, fragile, sick people—human beings twisted by their own personal histories.

We are all weak, wounded human beings, imperfect and full of defects—attempting to survive the difficulties of life and find a little peace and happiness.

Willingness to Forgive: Forgiveness is the release of others and the harm they have caused us. But forgiveness often follows deep acceptance of and repentance for our own harmful actions to others.

Acknowledging Our Powerlessness and Need for Healing Grace: We often feel powerless to name and accept the truth of the harm we have done. We likewise feel powerless to release the hurt others have done to us. This is especially true when dealing with deep pain. "[T]hough the decision to forgive must always come from within, we cannot change on our own strength. The power of forgiveness comes not from us, but from God. [God] can work in us only when we turn to [God] in prayer, trust, and humble recognition of our weaknesses."[37]

Am I willing to pray for the power:

- To ask for knowledge of the truth?

- To ask for freedom from the bondage of my own history?

- To wish for the spiritual healing of those persons or institutions that have harmed me?

- To forgive myself—to let go of self-condemnation, to let go of remorse, our temper, our addictions, our vanities, our arrogance, our smugness; to let go of our failures to do what we must and be who we are?

Am I willing to pray for the power:

- To love those who have hurt me as I love myself?

- To see the world and the people in it through the eyes of divine compassion?

Prayer. Inviting the healing power of God

- Into our minds—that our memories may be healed;

- Into our hearts—that our feelings may be healed;

- Into our souls—that our spirit may be healed and may flourish

We pray to the healing Spirit in the universe:

- Enable me to be willing to let go, to forgive, to release

- Enable me to be willing to find freedom

- Enable me to be willing to be restored to sanity

- Enable me to be willing to be taken to a place of serenity.

> Holy Spirit, enter the recesses of my heart, mind,
>   and soul
> and remove all traces of bitterness, anger and
>   resentment.
> Free me from feelings and grudges that steal my
>   energy and rob me of peace.
> Fill me with gratefulness for your merciful love and
>   help me to be an instrument of your healing
>   and forgiveness. Amen.

CHAPTER 6

Gateways to Gratitude

Make a joyful noise to the LORD, all the earth.
Worship the LORD with gladness;
Come into his presence with singing....
Enter his gates with thanksgiving...
Give thanks to him, bless his name.

—Ps 100:1–2, 4

WHEN WE HAVE CLEARED THE HURDLES of resentment and regret, we can more freely come into God's presence to give thanks. This chapter suggests two practices to guide our walk along the path of gratitude: deepening our appreciation for the blessings of each day and telling our life's story as a grace-filled tale.

DEEPENING OUR APPRECIATION

When you want very much something that you can have consider it a gift; accept it gracefully.[1]

The heart of appreciation is knowing what we value and sensing that we possess it in some real way. When we appreciate something—a person, an experience, an occasion, or an object—we acknowledge that it is of value to us, and we feel positively connected to it. Deepening our appreciation for what we already have been given is an important step toward living more gratefully. The saying "familiarity breeds contempt" may exaggerate the effect of getting accustomed to what we experience, but familiarity, in fact, does breed "habituation," the term positive psychologists use to describe how our appreciation of anything diminishes as we get used to it. After awhile, we start to take things for granted. Because of this human tendency, keeping a keen sense of appreciation for the cornucopia of created goods that surround us is an ongoing challenge. Appreciation and gratitude are vitally linked. The deeper our appreciation, the greater our gratitude. What follows are some ways of cultivating appreciation, an important prelude to gratitude.

Rekindling Wonder

Fostering appreciation begins with expanding a sense of wonder, with seeing commonly taken-for-granted things with fresh eyes, as Patricia Schneider's poem, "The Patience of Ordinary Things" delightfully illustrates:

It is a kind of love, is it not?
How the cup holds the tea,
How the chair stands sturdy and foursquare,
How the floor receives the bottoms of shoes or toes.
How soles of feet know where they're supposed
    to be.
I've been thinking about the patience of ordinary
    things,
How clothes wait respectfully in closets
And soap dries quietly in the dish,
And towels drink the wet from the skin of the back.
And the lovely repetition of stairs.
And what is more generous than a window?[2]

Gazing with wonder at all of creation entails seeing everyday things with appreciative eyes. An appreciative posture can take the form of standing in awe before the dazzling colors of a rose garden or the majestic shapes of Yosemite's stone monuments; it can occur when taking delight in a sunset or marveling over the beauty of a clear blue sky. A colorful illustration of wonder is the incident recounted in Nikos Kazantzakis' *Zorba the Greek.* One day, Zorba was riding on a donkey with his boss. As they passed an oncoming traveler on another donkey, Zorba's eyes were transfixed on the stranger. When chided by his companion for gawking so rudely at someone, Zorba proclaimed with childlike simplicity his amazement that there are such things as asses! Alexis Zorba's stance of amazement before daily realities, hardly noticed by most people, impressed his friend and narrator of the novel:

> I felt, as I listened to Zorba, that the world was recovering its pristine freshness. All the dulled daily things regained the brightness they had in the beginning, when we came out of the hands of God. Water, women, the stars, bread, returned to their mysterious, primitive origin and the divine whirlwind burst once more upon the air.[3]

To view ordinary things with astonishment—as if seeing them for the first time—reflects a capacity for appreciation.

Wonder is radical amazement over the very existence of the material universe. In the words of the philosopher Wittgenstein, "It is not *how* things are in the world that is mystical, but *that* it exists."[4] Radical amazement is caused by our "sense of perpetual surprise at the fact that there are facts at all."[5] A blade of grass, for example, does not contain its own adequate explanation or necessary reason for existence. At one time, it did not exist and at another time, it will cease to exist. It need not be, yet it enjoys the gift of being. Wonder refers, then, not only to what we see, but also to the very act of seeing, as well as to our own selves who see and are amazed at our very ability to see. The question that confronts everyone who ponders the existence of being is "Why is there something rather than nothing?" From an ecotheological viewpoint, wonder naturally evokes gratitude. "The universe itself is so vast and mysterious," an ecotheologian writes, "that it is more than enough to induce in us that sense of awe and joyful gratitude that played such a role in past religious experience. The religious rituals of the future will celebrate the wonder of the universe and the mystery of life."[6] Wonder escorts us appreciatively and gratefully into the garden of creation and there to witness the presence of the divine, who at every moment sustains all things in existence. "God does not die on the day when we cease to believe in a personal deity," states Dag Hammarskjöld, "but we die on the day when our lives cease to be illuminated by the steady radiance, renewed daily, of a wonder, the source of which is beyond all reason."[7]

Appreciating Our Todays

From the rich storehouse of Twelve-Step spirituality comes a helpful reminder about the importance of living in the present.

Yesterday is history.
Tomorrow is a mystery.
Today is a gift.
That's why we call it the present.

A delightful conversation between Alice and the Queen in chapter 5 of *Through the Looking Glass and What Alice Found There* points amusingly to the importance of cherishing each day as a wonderful gift and opportunity. Alice starts:

"I don't care for jam."

"It's very good jam," said the Queen

"Well, I don't want any *to-day*, at any rate."

"You couldn't have it if you *did* want it," the Queen said. "The rule is, jam to-morrow and jam yesterday—but never jam *to-day*."

"It *must* come sometimes to 'jam to-day,' " Alice objected.

"No, it can't," said the Queen. "It's jam every *other* day: to-day isn't any *other* day, you know."[8]

Surely, to live with a heightened sense that today isn't just any other day would greatly enlarge our appreciation for bread and breath, as well as all the other blessings that daily come our way. Or as Mary Oliver puts it with poetic vividness:

Of course for each of us, there is the daily life.
Let us live it, gesture by gesture.
When we cut the ripe melon, should we not give it
    thanks?
And should we not thank the knife also?
We do not live in a simple world.[9]

The call to treasure the "today" of our lives finds clear resonance in Luke's Gospel, which pronounces "today" as a special time of grace. In four different Lucan passages, "today" marks the announcement of the good news. Early in the Gospel, we hear the angels announcing tidings of great joy because "to you is born this day in the city of David a Savior" (2:11). When Jesus inaugurated his public ministry in Nazareth, he entered the synagogue on a Sabbath. After reading the scroll of the prophet Isaiah that was handed to him, Jesus ended by exclaiming, "Today this scripture has been fulfilled in your hearing" (4:21). "Today salvation has come to this house," Jesus told Zacchaeus, the senior tax collector who was too short to see above the crowd and had climbed a sycamore tree to get a glimpse of Jesus passing by (19:9). And finally, to the good thief hanging next to him on the cross, Jesus spoke words of consolation: "Today, you will be with me in Paradise" (23:43).

While living "today" as fully as we can increases our ability to appreciate, the tempo of modern life challenges our ability to live with a sense of wonder. Obstacles arise from simply being part of a culture that puts a premium on productivity and performance and often views leisure as a waste of time. This attitude is captured in a *Los Angeles Times* article entitled, "Blackberries Don't Fit in Bikinis."

> It's vacation prime time. Millions of wage-earners are on the road, in the air or on the water in search of overdue recreation, relaxation and adventure. But for too many, it will be a futile quest, thanks to a big, fat killjoy stowed away on the trip: OCP, or obsessive-compulsive productivity, a frantic fixation to wring results from every minute of the day, even our play.[10]

Impatient with a leisurely pace, regarding anything less than instant response as unnecessary delay, our action-oriented society can cause a restless anxiousness in us. These cultural attitudes undermine living with wonder and appreciation.

"Why do you not know how to interpret the present time?" (Luke 12:56). In this question, Jesus can be heard to be saying, according to Mary Marrocco, a contemporary spiritual writer, "Make the best of the time you have....Don't wait till you get there, settle now. Look at what is in front of you, and pay attention to what it says." She illustrates the importance of this message by recounting an incident that occurred in Washington, DC, in the winter of 2006. Joshua Bell, one of America's great professional violinists participated in an experiment. On his own

Stradivarius, he played six of the world's best classical pieces, while standing at a subway station. A video recording of the entire experiment, which lasted forty-three minutes, shows that every single child who passed by wanted to stop, but was hurried on by the accompanying adult. "What if everything our hearts are seeking," she reflects, "is available right where we are trying to escape from—here? In the moment we are trying to get away from—now?"[11] Our controlling, time-obsessed, ever-hurried culture can clearly benefit from the advice of Jesus to live with eyes open to the unfolding richness of our present experience. "Clock-consciousness" chokes off appreciation, which requires the ability to momentarily forget time and be enthralled by what is happening in the here-and-now.

In a similar vein, Rabbi Harold Kushner reflects on the folly of pursuing happiness with such a myopic fixation on the future that we are unable to enjoy the goods and blessings of the present. In *When All You've Ever Wanted Isn't Enough,* he shares:

> A rabbi once asked a prominent member of his congregation, "Whenever I see you, you're always in a hurry. Tell me, where are you running all the time?" The man answered, "I'm running after success, I'm running after fulfillment, I'm running after the reward for all my hard work."
>
> The rabbi responded, "That's a good answer if you assume that all those blessings are somewhere ahead of you, trying to elude you and if you run fast enough, you may catch up with them. But isn't it possible that those blessings are behind you, that they are looking for you, and the more you run, the harder you make it for them to find you?" Isn't it possible indeed that God has all sorts of wonderful presents for us—good food and beautiful sunsets and flowers budding in the spring and leaves turning in the fall and quiet

moments of sharing—but we in our pursuit of happiness are so constantly on the go that He (sic) cannot find us at home to deliver them?[12]

If we find ourselves caught up in a hectic lifestyle, we need to find ways to raise our awareness of what is going on around us and within us, right here and right now. Our appreciation for the gifts and blessings of ordinary life will grow in surprising ways, if we merely look at reality in a wide-eyed way.

To [someone] who hesitated to embark on the spiritual quest for fear of the effort and renunciation the Master said:

"How much effort and renunciation does it take to open one's eyes and see?"[13]

Silent Reflection Deepens Appreciation

As a doorway to awareness, silence has been valued through the centuries because of its spiritual fruitfulness. One of the most important fruits of silence is presence, which is synonymous with mindfulness. Presence is the capacity to simply be wholly where we are, totally engaged in the moment, with the people and work that are before us. We all need zones of quiet in order to deepen our appreciation for the gifts that fill our lives. But the silence must be more than a linguistic asceticism of not talking. More importantly, it must quiet our "monkey mind," the constant inner chatter that interrupts our focus and competes for our attention. A contemporary writer gives a colorful account of the struggle with this disruptive "monkey mind."

Like most humanoids, I am burdened with what the Buddhists call the "money mind"—the thoughts that swing from limb to limb, stopping only to scratch themselves, spit and howl. From the distant past to the unknowable future, my mind swings wildly through time, touching on dozens of ideas a minute, unharnessed and undisciplined. This in itself is not necessarily a problem; the problem is the emotional attachment that goes along with the thinking. Happy thoughts make me happy, but—*whoops!*—how quickly I swing again into obsessive worry, blowing the mood; and then it's the remembrance of an angry moment and I start to get hot and pissed off all over again; and then my mind decides it might be a good time to start feeling sorry for itself, and loneliness follows promptly. You are, after all, what you think. Your emotions are the slaves to your thoughts, and you are the slave to your emotions.

The other problem with all this swinging through the vines of thought is that you are never where you *are*. You are always digging in the past or poking at the future, but rarely do you rest in this moment. It's something like the habit of my dear friend Susan, who—whenever she sees a beautiful place—exclaims in near panic, "It's so beautiful here! I want to come back here someday!" and it takes all of my persuasive powers to try to convince her that she is *already* here. If you're looking for union with the divine, this kind of forward/backward whirling is a problem. There's a reason they call God a *presence*—because God is right *here* and right *now*. In the present is the only place to find Him, and now is the only time.[14]

Silence empties out the cup of consciousness, making us more open and receptive to all that life has to give.

Humility Deepens Appreciation

Humility counteracts narcissistic entitlement, which is one of the major enemies of gratitude. When we feel entitled to something, we are not prone to be grateful. After all, a sense of entitlement says that we have it coming to us; it's due us for one reason or another. "Spoiled children," for example, are grossly unappreciative because they believe that they are entitled to everything they receive. Humility, on the contrary, opens our hearts to gratitude by reminding us that every thing around us is a "gift," which we do not necessarily "deserve" or are "entitled to." In biblical spirituality, humility flows from the first beatitude: "Blessed are you who are poor, for yours is the kingdom of God" (Luke 6:20). To be poor in spirit is to acknowledge with Job that naked we came into the world and naked we will leave it. Thus, we pray, "Blessed be the name of the Lord," feeling grateful for whatever we have. Humility grounds us in the truth of who we are as dependent beings and enables us to acknowledge our reliance on God and others. Peaceful acceptance of our built-in limits as human beings allows us to affirm the goodness of life. Far from shrinking in shame, those who are poor in spirit turn to God with gratefulness and trust, knowing that the God who takes care of the birds of the sky and the lilies of the field is also the generous Giver of all that we need. Humility conditions us to be grateful recipients of God's bountiful love. The more humble we are, the more appreciative we will be for everything.

If there is an antidote to ingratitude, it is admitting that we can't make it on our own. The things we need to survive and flourish are simply not in our total control. Poverty of spirit invites us to face up to this reality and to accept the fact that fear is our lifetime companion as vulnerable creatures. "Our fears are a given, a part of our humanity. Instead of trying to control our fears, we need to pray out of the depths of them, to embrace our poverty of spirit, our continual need for strength and reassurance."[15]

Spiritual and Psychological Practices to Foster Appreciation

Rituals

Spiritual rituals such as saying grace before meals provide a practical way of punctuating our day with intentional moments of focused appreciation and gratitude. Thanking God and those who provide for our bodily needs on a regular basis sustains an appreciative disposition in us. The British writer G. K. Chesterton extends the practice of "saying grace" to include other events of his day.

> You say grace before meals. All right. But I say grace before the concert and the opera, and grace before the play and pantomime, and grace before I open a book, and grace before sketching, painting, swimming, fencing, boxing, walking, playing, dancing and grace before I dip the pen in the ink. (www.goodreads.com/quotes/show/12207)

Chesterton's practice of saying grace continually throughout the day invites us to consider how we might similarly ritualize our gratitude each day.

Communal rituals that celebrate birthdays, anniversaries of wedding and deaths, religious feast days, and civic holidays also break our routines in ways that provide opportunities to deepen appreciation. "Rituals allow us to express the deepest levels of our memories," writes pastoral theologian Kathleen Fischer, "and it is therefore especially important at times of joy and celebration, as well as loss and death."[16] When we celebrate a birthday, we acknowledge the blessing of the gift of our life or how the gift of someone else's life has enriched ours. Anniversaries of wedding and the death of loved ones refresh our appreciation for the gift of faithful companionship and love through the years. Communal rituals are important because they "can help us establish profound emotional connections in terms of our identities as individuals and members of families."[17] In addition, civic holidays, like the Fourth of July and Veterans' Day, provide not only time off from work, but a chance to deepen our awareness of the blessings we enjoy as a nation, in which our inalienable rights to life, liberty, and the pursuit of happiness are protected by the Constitution. Conscious and active participation in the rituals that accompany these occasions can deepen our appreciation.

For Christians who belong to a mainline liturgical tradition, the celebration of the Eucharist is the principal ritual of thanksgiving. The Prefaces that introduce the different Eucharistic Prayers serve as preludes or catalysts for thanksgiving by calling to mind the many gifts of God and stirring up gratitude in our hearts. Preface I for Christmas illustrates how the Preface functions as a buildup for the great thanksgiving prayer of the Eucharist.

> Father, all-powerful and ever-living God,
> we do well always and everywhere to give
> you thanks through Jesus Christ our Lord.
>
> In the wonder of the incarnation
> your eternal Word has brought to the eyes of faith
> a new and radiant vision of your glory.
> In him we see our God made visible
> and so are caught up in love of the God we cannot
>   see.
>
> And so, with all the choirs of angels in heaven
> we proclaim your glory
> and join in the unending hymn of praise.

Here the focus of our gratitude is the gift of the incarnation, when the Word of God became flesh in the person of Jesus Christ. Through the incarnation, the invisible Mystery of God becomes visible in the person of Jesus and enables us to have an experiential knowledge of the divine. As the author of the First Letter of John gratefully proclaims, "We declare to you what was from the beginning, what we have heard, what we have seen with our eyes, what we have looked at and touched with our hands, concerning the word of life—this life was revealed, and we have seen it and testify to it...so that our joy may be complete" (1 John 1:1–2, 4). Christian gratitude centers on the gift of this wonderful access to God through Jesus. In other Prefaces, we give thanks for the wide spectrum of God's gifts to humankind—the gifts of creation, as well as the gift of saving love made manifest in the life, death, and resurrection of Jesus. Thus, the Eucharist is a sweeping expression of appreciation for all of God's gifts.

Social and Self Comparisons

Comparing our situation to others who are less fortunate is another way of reviving a sense of appreciation that may have gone stale or dormant. Positive psychologists refer to this as "downward comparison." Downward social comparison can be especially helpful to those of us for whom "the habit of thinking about what's right is so non-ingrained that the way you get there is thinking about what's not wrong."[18] Comparing ourselves with those who are worse off can improve our ability to see what is good in our lives. Passing the wreckage of a traffic accident, for example, can trigger a spurt of appreciation for one's safety on the freeway; grief at losing one's home in a wind-driven brush fire can be mitigated in learning that others not only lost their homes, but also their lives. In comparison, one's suffering is relativized and there is deep gratitude that one's loved ones are alive and well.

Appreciation can also be built up through self-comparisons. Sometimes when reflecting on our present situation in the context of where we once were, we are struck with how far we have come! Recognition of achievements and accomplishments can deepen our appreciation for how we have grown and developed over time, as well as for those who have supported us along the way. For example, a recent physical exam shows significant improvement in our cholesterol, and we feel grateful for the gift of good health, whereas when we hear that the good health we are used to remains unchanged, we may be less inclined to appreciate this as a gift, because we take it for granted. Using downward social and self-comparisons as reference points when assessing our life is thus a useful way of building up appreciation.

Focusing on the Positives: This practice for heightening appreciation can focus on the past or on the present. Whichever our focus, the important thing is that we focus on what we *have* rather than on what we lack. Regarding our past, remembering happy moments can increase our appreciation for life. Fischer offers helpful guidelines for praying over the joyful mysteries as a way of recalling how our lives have been blessed.

> Open the album of your life. There you will find scenes in which you felt deeply loved or in which you knew joy; a wedding day, your family together for a holiday, your birthday celebrated with friends. Choose one of these joyful mysteries of your life. Take some time to recapture the original scene and the feelings that accompanied it. How was this love shown to you? By whom? What produced the joy in you? Call up the scene again in detail and let yourself experience some of the love and joy you felt when the event first took place. The work of memory is not simply recalling old dates, names, and places. It is the reawakening of those moments.[19]

From the repertory of positive psychology, we can borrow two practices that can help us focus on present reasons for being grateful. One is simply taking time out to record the things we are thankful for in a daily gratitude journal. This intentional recall of the blessings of the day has the effect of sharpening our perception of good things that occur and deepening our appreciation through the simple act of reliving them in memory. Another practice entails writing a gratitude letter and making a gratitude visit. Psychiatrist Irvin Yalom recounts how powerful this exercise can be. At a workshop conducted by Martin Seligman, one of the leaders of the positive psychology movement, Yalom was directed to:

> Think of someone still living toward whom you feel great gratitude that you have never expressed. Spend ten minutes writing that person a gratitude letter and then pair up with someone here, and each of you read your letter to the other. The final step is that you pay a personal visit to that person sometime in the near future and read that letter aloud.

Yalom recounts the emotional impact that the exercise had on the participants:

> After the letters were read in pairs, several volunteers were selected from the audience to read their letters aloud to the entire audience. Without exception, each person choked up with emotion during the reading. I learned that such displays of emotion invariably occur in this exercise: very few participants get through the reading without being swept by a deep emotional current.[20]

TELLING THE STORY OF OUR LIFE
AS A GRACE-FILLED TALE

O give thanks to the LORD, call on his name,
> make known his deeds among the peoples.
Sing to him, sing praises to him;
> tell of all his wonderful works....
Remember the wonderful works he has done...
He is mindful of his covenant forever...
> (Ps 105:1–2, 5, 8).

When we recall the names, dates, and events that fill the seasons of our lives and put all that information into a narrative structure, we are telling our life story. We frame the facts of our life into a story in order to provide meaning and coherence to what would otherwise be a jumble of disconnected recollections. Autobiographies take various forms. Some convey the tale of their life as a story of empowerment and early defining moments, for example, President Barack Obama's *The Audacity of Hope*; others, like Elizabeth Edwards in both her memoirs, *Saving Grace* and *Resilience*, reconfigure the constellation of their experiences and narrate a story of loss and difficulties that have shaped their lives. It is possible to tell our stories in many ways. However, if we frame and tell our story to ourselves and others in a way that highlights how the faithful love of God has blessed us from our mother's womb, we cannot escape the fact that our lives have been "full of grace." Hence, an important gateway to increased gratitude is to tell our life story as a story of grace. Telling our story is spiritually fruitful because "Stories are the carriers, the containers for our most sacred and powerful understandings of the self and of God."[21]

We speak of "grace" here, not in an abstract theological way, but as the concrete and tangible ways that the love of God has spilled into creation and flowed into our lives, sometimes in

167

mysterious, but always in life-giving ways. Grace, a contemporary spiritual writer perceptively points out, "includes unmerited favor, forgiveness, second-chances, surprises, reframings, epiphanic breakthroughs, whole paradigm shifts. It is a word that reaffirms the gift character of all that we are and have. It is an organizing force in every life story."[22] By telling our story as a grace-filled tale, we intentionally focus our attention on all the people and events through which our lives have been touched by grace and laced with the provident care of a loving God. With the lens of faith, we can review our history with a keen eye in search of the myriad ways God has blessed us with amazing grace. Such a prayerful look at our life can help us recognize in the ordinary course of our days the surprises and "unmerited gifts, the goodness that arises from the ash heap of failure, the joy that comes in the wake of loss, the times when God breaks through the logic of circumstance and ambushes us with love and with new opportunities."[23] A grateful look at our life will convince us of the truth of the biblical proclamation that "From his fullness we have all received, grace upon grace" (John 1:16).

The Parable of the Treasure and the Pearl

In one short verse, Matthew (13:44–45) presents us with two parables that, at first glance, look like two accounts of a single message: God is the answer to our heart's deepest desire and it is worth giving up everything we have in order to have God as the center of our life. A closer look, however, reveals a striking difference in the two accounts. The first account tells us "the kingdom of heaven is like treasure hidden in a field, which someone *found....*" The treasure is something that this fortunate person stumbles onto, a wonderful surprise that he trips over as he makes his way through life. The second account, however, says that the kingdom of heaven is like a merchant's search for fine pearls. Finding the precious pearl, for which he sells everything he has in order to possess, is the result of *a deliberate search.*[24]

The first account refers to inadvertently finding something so valuable and precious that it becomes central to our life and anchors our joy in living. It is a stark reminder that so much of what grounds our happiness is gift, something that we have not deliberately sought out, but have surprising found. And, with marvelous delight, we thank God. To expand our gratitude, we might reflect prayerfully on the hidden treasures that we have found through life.

- What are moments when you have been surprised by joy?

- Have there been moments when you experienced unexpected harmony, when everything in life seemed to fit together?

- Reflecting on the experience of meeting your spouse, discovering your life's work or witnessing the birth of your child can also strike you with wondrous gratitude.

Such experiences should evoke in us a heartfelt realization that all is gift. We are not in control of life, but the reign of God is the gracious source of the many blessings we discover in life. Like the person in the parable who makes such a rich find, we too must value these blessings wholeheartedly.

In writing up your life story as a tale of grace, try to remember people and events that evoke gratitude, such as when you experienced:

- Second chances

- Forgiveness

- Joyful surprises

- Liberating epiphanies and transforming insights, "aha moments"

- Life-changing paradigm shifts

- Unmerited gifts

- Random kindness

- Good arising from failure and misfortune

- Unexpected joy that came in the wake of loss

- Unexpected doors opening, opportunities that defied the logic of circumstances

Stories of grace tell of both dramatic and mundane encounters. Examples of dramatic occasions for gratitude are reported regularly in the media, such as the following story of survivors of a tornado whose town was decimated in a matter of minutes gathering together to share their loss as well as their gratitude for having been spared. On Friday, May 4, 2007, a powerful twister leveled more than 90 percent of the town of Greensburg, Kansas, about 110 miles west of Wichita and home to about 1,400 people. After a mere thirty-minute warning, the fierce tornado flattened homes and businesses, killing nine people and injuring fifty—wiping out an entire community. No wonder those who survived found reason to be grateful, even in the midst of the devastation.[25] In less dramatic form, grace works in subtler ways in daily life: for example, when we encounter the forgiveness of a loved one for a wrong committed; when we are surprised by the steady support of faithful friends in the aftermath of a terminal diagnosis and imminent death; or when we hear a reconciling word of heartfelt gratitude from a son or daughter, whose silence over the years expressed resentment for painful childhood memories. Our tale of grace is richer when it includes both the dramatic and the ordinary!

The Old Testament can be seen as the faith autobiography of Israel. As literature, it is not strictly history, but rather religious testimony. The writers of the Old Testament were more concerned with telling their "salvation history" than with giving an objective chronicle of historical events. They wanted to proclaim how God's faithfulness endured through the thick-and-thin of their messy history, with its brief moment of glory under King David, long years of infidelity to God, of defeat, humiliation, and captivity. In short, the Old Testament recounts the salvation history of our spiritual ancestors. Its central purpose is to proclaim and celebrate the "great acts of God" on Israel's behalf in order to arouse in us a grateful and loving response to the God of the Exodus who remains the Holy One in our midst today. In a similar way, our own autobiography, by knitting together our experiences in the light of God's faithfulness to us, makes up our personal "salvation history." Getting in touch with God's goodness to us in the past is a way of deepening our trust in God's presence today. Like the Israelites who "dis-membered" (took apart) the events of their past in order to "re-member" it (put it back together) in the light of God's caring presence, we too benefit by telling our life story with God's faithful love as the unifying theme.

Looking Back with Gratitude

Research shows, according to positive psychologist Philip Watkins, that a strong link exists between recalling positive experiences and our present capacity to experience happiness. Gratitude benefits us not only by helping us appreciate the good things that happen to us when they occur, but also by embedding them in our memories. Gratitude enhances happiness, states Watkins, because "[a] more grateful person should be more likely to notice positive aspects in his or her life and thus enhance the encoding of these experiences in memory."[26] In other words, when we are disposed to being grateful, the favors we receive catch our attention in a way that stores them more securely in our memory. Thus, "grateful individuals should be more likely to recall past benefits from their life and to experience gratitude in response to these blessings."[27] This psychological finding is expressed with poetic vividness below:

> Something seen, something heard, something felt, flashes upon one with a bright freshness, and the heart, tired or sick or sad or merely indifferent, stirs and lifts in answer. Different things do it for different people, but the result is the same: that fleeting instant when we lose ourselves in joy and wonder. It is minor because it is slight and so soon gone; it is an ecstasy because there is an impersonal quality in the vivid thrust of happiness we feel, and because the stir lingers in the memory.[28]

By enabling us to access positive memories more readily, gratitude contributes to our happiness by helping us to better cope with unpleasant situations and feelings. For example, while suffering the death of lifelong friends—a painful aspect of aging—positive memories can sustain us in our loss. "This is where memory helps," a writer on aging and spiritual growth states, "and why old people treasure it so much. It is a kind of hump in which we store recollections of happiness, of being loved, of people and places that were dear to us, of pleasure and success in work, of the joys of child-rearing."[29] The contents of the "hump of memory" are especially consoling when we are struggling with sadness, fear, and self-doubt.

In the same vein, Cistercian monk Basil Pennington counts having the leisure to remember friendships and positive life events as one of the blessings of growing older and slowing down. Even though he finds himself spending more time alone, loved ones are "so present in the spirit, in the reality of memory, in the books of pictures I take out and leaf through. We are together again in wonderful moments of life," he states. "And they can be savored in a way that they could not be when they were rushing by in the midst of so many doings. Yes, there are the painful, the sad, the sorrowful memories. But I have the right to choose. I can 'flip the channel' and dwell with the memories of my choice, although at times it is consoling to hold again some painful moments, to hold them before God in healing and prayerful love."[30]

In a brief account of her own "salvation history," church historian and spiritual writer Roberta Bondi "dis-members" both the happy and painful memories of life and "re-members" them, weaving a story of her life as a tale of grace. As with the Israelites of old, God's unconditional love provides the unifying framework for her story. When she was a little girl, despair pervaded her, making her fear that even at age twenty-five she would never be "an ordinary, powerful, confident, self-sufficient, outgoing, competent grown-up who actually talked to other grown-ups."[31] And her childhood fears seemed to have come true, for at twenty-five, her experience of her life matched her worst fears.

> I didn't feel powerful; in fact, I hardly felt in control of my life at all. Whether I was pleasing my husband caused me great anxiety. I worried constantly about meeting other people's expectations and I sought their approval compulsively. I rarely experienced myself as competent. I continued to suffer from shyness as well as the dependent loneliness of childhood, and trying to talk to adults even a little older than I was excruciating.[32]

Yet years later, she is able to proclaim with grateful wonderment, "It would have seemed impossible then [at age twenty-five] that

I should look back over my life from where I am now and not only know that it is a good thing to be fifty-five, but also be glad that there is no one on earth whose life I would trade for mine."[33]

In sharing what has made aging so much more wonderful than she thought it could be, Bondi recounts the many blessings of her life: "an exceptional husband who is my companion in every way," children, a mother, friends, and students whom she enjoys and loves and who reciprocate in kind. She also mentions the blessing that the women's movement has been for her in opening doors of opportunity for rich and rewarding engagement outside the home in meaningful work. But above and beyond anything else, what has enabled her to recount the story of her life as a grateful tale is the abiding love of God, something she "only had glimpses of in my twenties." In intimate terms, she shares what has made all the difference in the world for her:

> It is a knowledge of my own grounding in God, who over the years has slowly, steadily freed me from both debilitating perfectionism and guilt, and from the energy-sapping burden of trying to please everybody I know in both my personal and professional lives. This grounding in God continues to give me the strength to discern, work, and suffer for what I myself value. At the same time, it has increasingly allowed me a space to confront and be confronted by my own wounds to my ability to love and receive love and to seek healing from God.[34]

Memory Keeps God's Presence Alive

Remembering God's faithfulness to us in the past is an important way of staying hopeful in the present. When we forget how God has come through for us before, we are less able to trust God's presence in our current struggles. That is why the Old Testament continually encourages us to remember God's commitment of fidelity. After being rescued from the flood, Noah was given the rainbow as a sign of the ongoing and caring presence of God.

> God said, "This is the sign of the covenant that I make between me and you and every living creature that is with you, for all future generations: I have set my bow in the clouds, and it shall be a sign of the covenant between me and the earth....When the bow is in the clouds, I will see it and remember the everlasting covenant between God and every living creature of all flesh that is on the earth" (Gen 9:12–13, 16).

Rainbows are meant to remind us that God is always nearby.

Forgetfulness of God's caring intervention on their behalf frequently caused our spiritual ancestors to stray and to lose hope in God's faithfulness. As the Book of Judges states, Israel relapsed into idolatry because "The Israelites did not remember the LORD their God, who had rescued them from the hand of all their enemies on every side" (8:34). This spiritual amnesia led to their inability to trust in God in the present. Attempting to revive their waning faith, prophets would rise up and challenge them to remember God's concrete acts of fidelity in their history: "Remember that you were a slave in the land of Egypt, and the LORD your God brought you out from there with a mighty hand and an outstretched arm" (Deut 5:15). Remember today that it was you who have known and seen

> ...his mighty hand and his outstretched arm, his signs and his deeds that he did in Egypt to Pharaoh, the king of Egypt, and to all his land; what he did to the Egyptian army, to their horses and chariots, how he made the

water of the Red Sea flow over them as they pursued you, so that the LORD has destroyed them to this day; what he did to you in the wilderness, until you came to this place...for it is your own eyes that have seen every great deed that the Lord did (Deut 11:2–6, 7).

Do not be afraid of them [the foreign nations who outnumber Israel]. Just remember what the LORD your God did to Pharaoh and to all Egypt, the great trials that your eyes saw, the signs and wonders, the mighty hand and the outstretched arm by which the LORD your God brought you out. The LORD your God will do the same to all the peoples of whom you are afraid (Deut 7:18–19).

Forgetfulness causes us to doubt God's caring presence in our lives; remembering God's past acts of loving kindness fuels our faith.

Prayer as Recall and Reminiscence

A middle-aged man named Charles, given to increasing memory lapses (what he euphemistically refers to as "senior moments"), was heard bragging to Henry, a childhood friend.

Charles: "Henry, you won't believe this fantastic clinic I've discovered to improve my memory. The place is staffed with experts who give us all kinds of techniques and aids to improve our memory."
Henry: "That sounds great. What's the name of the place?"
Charles: "They teach us how to use mnemonic devices and drill us in practice sessions. It's been really helpful."

Henry: "What's the name of the place?"

Charles: "My recall of names and dates has improved tremendously."

Henry: "Well what's the name of the place?"

Charles: "Well, first let me ask you a question. What's the name of the plant with bright colored flowers and thorns on the stems?"

Henry: "A rose."

Charles: (turning to his wife) "Rose, what's the name of that place?"

Because memory loss is a normal part of aging, a spiritual discipline that involves periodically calling to mind God's concrete blessings in the unfolding of our life story is important for spiritual vitality. This can take the form of writing a faith or spiritual autobiography, in which we recount the "stepping stones" that have led us to where we are in the present. Some helpful questions in telling the story of God's presence in our life are:

- What have been significant events in my life?

- Who have been important people in my life?

- How have I experienced God in the different stages of my life and development?

- In what ways in my life have I experienced the giving and receiving of love, affirmation, forgiveness, healing, and freedom?

- What biblical images or stories reflect how God has been part of my life?

Before trying to put any order to this spiritual autobiography, it is helpful to jot down memories from childhood and recent years, just as they come to awareness. Later, these memories can be organized into a personal story of our life with God. This exercise helps us to get in touch with our history and recognize how God's presence weaves itself through the events of our lives. The ability to remember is an essential aspect of grateful living. It allows us to cherish important persons and significant events of the past and to prolong our appreciation of them in the present.

Looking Back to Understand the Footprints in the Sand

Memory enables us to recall moments when we experienced the help of God during difficult times. Recalling those graced times expands our capacity to trust that God is still with us, even though we might not feel it at the moment. Sometimes it is only with hindsight that we see how God has been with us all along. Once, Moses said to God:

> "Show me your glory, I pray." And [God] said "I will make all my goodness pass before you, and will proclaim before you the name, 'The LORD'; and I will be gracious to whom I will be gracious, and will show mercy on whom I will show mercy. But," he said, "you cannot see my face; for no one shall see me and live." And the LORD continued "See, there is a place by me where you shall stand on the rock; and while my glory passes by I will put you in a cleft of the rock, and I will cover you with my hand until I have passed by; then I will take away my hand, and you shall see my back; but my face shall not be seen" (Exod 33:18–23).

It has been suggested that the Hebrew word, *achorai*, translated as God's "back" in this passage, would be more spiritually insightful if translated as God's "afterwards," for it is often later, after God has passed by, that we recognize how the glory of God has graced our lives.[35] The popular reflection, "Footprints," reflects this biblical truth.

> One night a man had a dream. He dreamed he was walking along the beach with the Lord. Across the sky flashed scenes from his life. For each scene, he noticed two sets of footprints in the sand: one belonging to him, and the other to the Lord.
>
> When the last scene of his life flashed before him, he looked back at the footprints in the sand. He noticed that many times along the path of his life there was only one set of footprints. He also noticed that it happened at the very lowest and saddest times in his life.
>
> This really bothered him and he questioned the Lord about it. "Lord, you said that once I decided to follow you, you'd walk with me all the way. But I have noticed that during the most troublesome times in my life, there is only one set of footprints. I don't understand why when I needed you most you would leave me."
>
> The Lord replied, "My child, my precious child, I love you and I would never leave you. During your times of trial and suffering, when you see only one set of footprints, it was then that I carried you."[36]

Thus, the mystery of the disappearing footprints is solved. At times of crises, we are not abandoned, but rather carried by God. This consoling insight, however, may come only in retrospect, when our eyes are opened to see God's "afterwards." With patience, we are called to hold in memory our dark and desolate experiences of the past until grace gradually illuminates how God has always been in those painful places; with this realization can come much consolation and healing. Memory serves us well when it makes us mindful of the enduring presence of a God who promises to walk always with us. But, even if our memory falters, the imprint on our hearts is lasting, as expressed so poignantly in the following poem:

> ...Joy came in the morning...
> and the storms in measure over,
> and the spring time came,
> and the singing of birds,
> and the voice of the Turtle is heard in our land.
> O! the glorious day that is dawned upon us,
> where the morning stars do sing together,
> and the sons and daughters of God
> do shout for joy...
> Oh God's tender dealings can never
> be erased from our remembering,
> for God has printed them in our hearts....[37]

❧ SPIRITUAL EXERCISES AND REFLECTIONS ❧

A Life Review Through the Prism of Gratitude[38]

Sit quietly and recall someone from your past whose kindness and care touched your heart. Imagine yourself in conversation with that person. Tell them how blessed you feel for the gift of their presence in your life and what they have meant to you. Send your gratitude to them as if your hearts were connected. Thank them, and when you are finished with the conversation, say a warm good-bye. Say farewell to them as if you might never see them again, even in memory.

In an unhurried way, call into mind, one by one, people who have supported you: parents, grandparents, friends, lovers, ministers, teachers, classmates, and colleagues. Share with each of them how grateful you are for their kindness and care. When you feel satisfied that you have expressed your love and gratitude to them, say good-bye as if you might never be this way again.

Every time you encounter in prayerful memory those whom you care for with gratitude, the experience changes lightly as the conversation unfolds under the influence of grace and the parting becomes less a separation than a completion.

As this gratitude-practice continues, expand your attention to include not only people, but also moments from the past for which you feel grateful. Recall those events when you felt blessed or graced and relive them with gratitude. Thank God for them.

A Grateful Testament of Your Life

Imagine that you are going to die today. You want to spend some time alone to write down for your friends a sort of testament for which the points that follow could serve as chapter titles.

- These things I have loved in life
- These things I have tasted
- These things I have looked at
- These things I have smelled
- These things I have heard
- These things I have touched
- These experiences I have cherished
- These ideas have brought me liberation
- These convictions I have lived by
- These things I have lived for
- These risks I took

- These sufferings have seasoned me
- These influences have shaped my life (persons, occupations, books, events)
- These scripture texts have lit my path
- These are my life's accomplishments
- These persons are enshrined in my heart[39]

CHAPTER 7

Ordinary Mysticism and Gratefulness

Mysticism is felt-gratitude for everything.
—ANTHONY DE MELLO[1]

"THE CHRISTIAN OF THE FUTURE will either be a mystic, one who has experienced something, or he will cease to be anything at all."[2] This provocative statement of Jesuit Karl Rahner, one of the leading Catholic theologians of the twentieth-century, may be confusing, even off-putting, to many. How can being a mystic be essential to being a Christian, when mysticism seems so unrelated to ordinary life? Furthermore, as biblical theologian Marcus Borg points out, the terms *mystics* and *mysticism* are "at best vague and often have negative connotations, suggesting fuzzy thinking or something that need not be taken seriously. And even when the terms are understood to refer to experiences of the sacred, they often suggest an otherworldly orientation that has little to do with the dailiness of life."[3] However, by "mysticism," Rahner does not mean "singular parapsychological phenomena, but a genuine experience of God emerging from the very heart of existence."[4] Mystics, therefore, are people who have firsthand experience of God from their own personal encounter. Merely being a member of a religion, Rahner asserts, is no longer sufficient today to maintain a vital faith. Neither the doctrinal knowledge received through one's religious upbringing, nor the vicariously shared experience of others, will be able to sustain one's faith in a vibrant way. According to Rahner, we must, have a personal and experiential basis for our beliefs as Christians. Not referring to otherworldly experiences, he was thinking of a "mysticism of daily life," which enables ordinary Christians, who are alert, awake, and attentive, to experience the movements of God's Spirit in the encounters of daily life. Like Brother David Steindl-Rast, who asserts that every human being is potentially a mystic, Rahner encourages all Christians to develop their mystic potential and to foster a faith that can illuminate reality in such a way that the gift-nature of everything shines forth. In this way, faith can draw us to God with gratitude and love.

THE MYSTICISM OF EVERYDAY LIFE

Rahner's notion of a "mysticism of everyday life" is essentially a stance of faith. When viewed with the eyes of faith, he states, "the very commonness of everyday things harbors the eternal marvel and silent mystery of God and his grace."[5] In this, Rahner reveals his Ignatian background. Ignatius took for granted that God is always present and at work for us. The spiritual challenge, according to him, is to recognize *how* and to respond with gratitude and openness. Defining "devotion" as the ease in finding God in all things," he valued prayer as a means of cultivating devotion. The prayer that is most characteristic of Ignatian spirituality is the awareness examen or the examination of consciousness. Ignatius considered the examen to be more important than lengthy meditation. Even when ill health necessitated the dropping of all other spiritual practices, he never dispensed his followers from doing it.

The examen carves out a few moments of solitude in the midst of a busy day to allow us to reflect on what is going on and where our actions and choices are taking us. It is a form of discernment, because it enables us to look concretely at events and ask:

- Where is God in *this* situation?

- How is God leading me?

- What is God saying to me?

- How was God there for me in *that* experience?

- What in my present situation is leading me to God and others in love?

- What is leading me away?

- What is the underlying spirit in my dealing with others?

- What is really going on in what's happening in my life these days?

Such questions invite us to find and respond to God in our concrete, daily experiences.

The examen enables us, with the help of God's illuminating grace, to stay in touch with the currents and undercurrents of our fast-paced lives. It is often difficult, at the actual time, to know what is really going on (meaning and significance) in what is taking place (occurrence or event). For example, imagine that you are at the airport and you notice a fight suddenly flare up between a husband and wife soon to be separated from one another. What you observe is that a conflict is occurring. But what is going on beneath the observable actions and words is not apparent. Perhaps, their fight manifests a struggle to let go of each other or an unconscious effort to ease the pain of imminent separation. Or perhaps it is a way of making contact after months of alienation and stony silence, since fighting is at least a form of contact. These possible explanations may be a truer picture of what is going on than the observable issue that sparked the conflict. Similarly, our interactions with people and our emotional responses to events often leave us wondering what's going on in ourselves. We need solitude and a contemplative distance to get the meaning and significance of our experiences. The awareness examen is a perspective-providing prayer that allows God's grace to illumine our hearts and minds.

The structure of the awareness examen can take various forms, but essentially consists of five steps (*Spiritual Exercises*, no. 43).

Step 1: Praying in gratitude for all the gifts that God has given us. Instead of taking the gifts of God for granted, we reflect on our many blessings. With an attitude of gratitude, we glance back at the past twenty-four hours, from hour to hour, from place to place, from event to event, from person to person, thanking God for every gift we have experienced. This reflective thanksgiving can lead eventually to a more spontaneous gratitude as we start to recognize these gifts throughout our day.

In his version of the Ignatian examen, which he describes as "Rummaging for God: Praying Backwards through Your Day," Jesuit scripture scholar Dennis Hamm comments:

> Note how different this is from looking immediately for your sins.
>
> Nobody likes to poke around in the memory bank to uncover smallness, weakness, lack of generosity. But everybody likes to fondle beautiful gifts, and that is precisely what the past twenty-four hours contain—gifts of existence, work, relationships, food, challenges. Gratitude is the foundation of our whole relationship with God. So use whatever cues help you to walk through the day from the moment of awakening—even the dreams you

recall upon awakening. Walk through the past twenty-four hours...thanking the Lord for every gift you encounter.[6]

Step 2: Praying for God's enlightenment so that the Spirit will help us see ourselves more clearly, freed from defensiveness and blind spots. Here we are praying for a Spirit-guided insight into our actions and our hearts. For example, we may pray for light to understand what is going on in a painful misunderstanding with our spouse, aging parent, close friend, co-worker, or teenager. This step of asking for God's assistance is critical because it distinguishes the awareness examen as a form of prayer from pure psychological introspection. Hamm makes this point when he states, "The goal is not simply memory but graced understanding. That's a gift from God devoutly to be begged. 'Lord, help me understand this blooming, buzzing confusion.' "[7]

Step 3: Surveying the day or the period since last doing the examen, paying attention to our feelings, moods, thoughts, and urgings as a way of getting a sense of what is going on in our lives. More often than not, our feelings—whether painful or pleasant, negative or positive—are the best indicators of what is happening in our lives and where we need to listen to the voice of God. In doing this step, it is important not to judge our feelings, but simply to acknowledge and accept them. Many of us were taught as children to consider certain feelings as good and acceptable and others as bad and unacceptable. The suppression of feelings that occurs because of this kind of judgmental attitude causes much loneliness and self-alienation. Spiritually, the rejection of feelings deadens our souls and blinds us to God's movements within.

As we simply pay attention to the whole range of feelings that surface when we welcome them into our consciousness, we ask ourselves: "What is the call or nudging of God in this feeling of anxiety, boredom, fear, anger, impatience, resentment, regret, shame, doubt, confusion, envy, confidence, attraction, delight, peace, desire, etc.?" As we stay with whatever feelings are most intense, we try to let our prayer be the spontaneous cry of our heart. The cry can be one of thanks and praise. Or it can be a cry for help and healing, for courage and strength.

Step 4: Praying for forgiveness for the ways we have not lived up to the requirements of love in our relationship to God, ourselves and others. The goal here is to glean the lessons of love embedded in yesterday's experiences and to move on with the new opportunities contained in the gift of tomorrow. It's important here not to let past failures impede our soulful engagement in the emerging present.

Step 5: Asking God's help to live with renewed hope and increased love of God and others. As we let our minds consider briefly what lies ahead in the immediate future (i.e., events, tasks, appointments), we pay attention to the feelings that spontaneously arise and share them with God in prayer, like one friend speaking to another.

Done at midday or before bed, the awareness exam can serve as a prayerful pause to remind us that God is with us in the activities of our busy days, as well as in the quiet moments we find for more lengthy formal prayer. Intended as a short prayer, between ten and fifteen minutes, the examen provides an ideal way of fostering gratitude on a daily basis.

Gratitude at Finding God at Home

Regular practice of the awareness examen can cultivate our ability to find God at home. God is "at home" in the sense that God is ever present and available, as well as in the sense that God can be found at home, where we live. A rabbinical story expresses well the truth that God is to be encountered where God has placed us, not in a heavenly city or special place.

In the hiddenness of time there was a poor man who left his village, weary of his life, longing for a place where he could escape all the struggles of this earth. He set out in search of a magical city—the heavenly city of his dreams, where all things would be perfect. He walked all day and by dusk found himself in a forest, where he decided to spend the night. Eating the crust of bread he had brought, he said his prayers and, just before going to sleep, placed his shoes in the center of the path, pointing them in the direction he would continue the next morning. Little did he imagine that while he slept, a practical joker would come along and turn his shoes around, pointing them back in the direction from which he had come.

The next morning, in all the innocence of folly, he got up, gave thanks to the Lord of the Universe, and started on his way again in the direction that his shoes pointed. For a second time he walked all day, and toward evening finally saw the magical city in the distance. It wasn't as large as he had expected. As he got closer, it looked curiously familiar. But he pressed on, found a street much like his own, knocked on a familiar door, greeted the family he found there— and lived happily ever after in the magical city of his dreams.[8]

Faith does not transport us to a magical city, but enables us to appreciate anew the rich blessings that are contained at home.

Finding God in All Things

Insisting on God's presence in all things, Ignatius once denied permission to a group of young Jesuit students who asked to prolong their morning meditation. Finding God in all things, instead of lengthy time in prayer, Ignatius responded, was to be their way to God. "They should strive to seek the presence of God our Lord in all things—for instance, in association with others, in walking, looking, tasting, hearing, thinking, indeed, in all that they do. It is certain that the majesty of God is in all things by God's presence, activity, and essence."[9] Thus, it is not surprising that the Jesuit Teilhard de Chardin once prayed, "Let us leave the surface and without leaving the world, plunge into God." Teilhard speaks of the radiance of the divine milieu, which changes nothing in the relationships between things, but bathes the world with an inward light that leads us to a sense of God's presence. We could say that the great mystery of Christian faith is not exactly the appearance, but the transparency of God in the universe. Or as the Jesuit poet Gerard Manley Hopkins puts it, God is to be recognized not in special visions, but in the way divinity will "flame out, like shining from shook foil" through all creation for all with eyes of faith to see.

Teilhard touched so many with his message, suggested a friend, because he knew how to make again of the universe a temple.[10] His deep faith in the abiding presence of God allowed him to pray, "Lord, grant that I may see, that I may see *You*, that I may see and feel You *present in all things and animating* all things."[11] In one of his most frequently anthologized poems, "Hurrahing in Harvest," Hopkins ponders the changing of the seasons and realizes that he had not truly been attentive to the glory around him. He writes, near the end of the poem, "These things, / these things were here and but the beholder / Wanting." The world is indeed "charged with the grandeur of God," but what is needed is someone to behold it. Without attentive awe and reverence, creation is often left without appreciative and grateful beholders. Sadly, too often creation has to play to an empty house.

Ordinary Mysticism: Beholding the Presence

According to William James, one of the defining characteristics of mystical experiences is that they are illuminating or enlightening. "Ordinary mystics" are regular people like us, who have a capacity to see reality in a new light. This capacity—paradoxically both a grace from God and a developed spiritual sensibility—transforms how we perceive life and respond to people and events. Mystical experiences can make the scales fall from our eyes and enable us to *see*. It can often lift the shroud of darkness and despair in painful situations, allowing light to bring hope. Apart from intense moments when we enjoy special brushes with the Holy, theologian Thomas Hart speaks of a "low level daily experience of God." These experiences invite us to respond with gratitude and love. According to Hart:

> We experience God wherever we experience goodness, beauty, or depth. Here God seems to be saying, "Let me give you a glimpse of what I am like." The response? "You are amazing. Thank you."
>
> We experience God wherever we come up against our limits: our smallness, powerlessness, bafflement, discontent, mortality. Here God seems to be saying, "It is I you are looking for. I am your salvation." The response? "Thank you. I do need you. I put my life in your hands." We experience God wherever we feel an inner nudge toward doing the good. Here God seems to be saying, "Just do it." The response? "I will."[12]

When we approach daily life with a contemplative attitude, grace enables us to perceive in the world intimations of the divine, to feel in the rush of the passing the stillness of the eternal, and to sense the ultimate in the simple, common, ordinary experiences of our lives. These moments of graced insight are experienced not as huge religious experiences, but more like "an 'eyelid blink' glimpse of a presence that is mysterious and wise, which draws me, just for a moment, to a deeper realm."[13] These epiphanies or glimpses of the divine in our midst can be touched off by such ordinary realities as "a tone of voice, a waft of music on an intercom system, a bird song, a profound or challenging remark, a leaf falling on the windshield, a slant of sunshine on a building, an unexpected smile of a stranger or a colleague, an envelope with familiar handwriting...."[14]

Ordinary mystics have a graced intuition that everything not only comes from God as gift, but that God dwells intimately in all that exists (*Spiritual Exercises*, nos. 234–5). Writing in her journal, a student in a course on Ignatian spirituality expresses with poetic beauty the faith of an ordinary mystic.

> God is the rain that pours down to nourish the earth,
>   and the rainbow arched across the sky after the
>   rain.
> God is the bud beginning to sprout from the soil and
>   the centuries-old Sequoia tree pointing toward
>   the endless sky.
> God is the waterfall, overflowing with life and love,
>   pouring it out for me beautifully and powerfully.
> God is the sparkle in my eye, the story behind my
>   smile, the melody in my laughter, and the
>   spring in my step.
> God is the outstretched hand, the warm embrace,
>   the pat on the back, the stroking of my hair, the
>   warmth of the sun on my skin.
> God is the knowing, the not knowing, and the want-
>   ing to know.
> God is passion, freedom, truth, beauty, and love.

God is a kind word on a rough day and a letter from
a loved one far away.

God is the familiarity of the now and the uncertainty
of the future.

God is home.

God is the friend who is always there for me, who
challenges me, believes in me, and loves me
fully for me.

God is the lucky break that I don't quite deserve but
am thankful for anyway.

God is food on the table, a new day of life, water for
a shower, clothes to wear, books to read, and a
bed to sleep in.

God is learning and teaching, running, playing,
singing and dancing.

God is friendship and a surprise phone call.

God is riding in the car with the windows down, wind
in my hair, singing to the radio.

God is the person I struggle to accept, struggle to
love, and struggle to appreciate.

God is the part of me that I struggle to accept,
struggle to love, and struggle to appreciate.

God is the pieces that seem to fall into place, and
those that fall out of place and make me search
for a better way.

God is the lesson in mistakes and the wisdom in
trials.

God is the letting go, the deepest desire.

God is my talents and gifts, my hands, my feet, my
voice, calling me to action—to serve, to live out
God's dream for me and the world.

God is the dreamer and the dream, the lover, the
beloved, the love.

Ordinary Mysticism and Gratefulness

Jesuit Anthony de Mello reveals his Ignatian roots when he states "mysticism is felt-gratitude for everything." Growing in gratefulness, according to Ignatian spirituality, requires us to spot the traces of grace that saturate our world, to recognize the concrete ways that grace abounds in our lives—in small and big ways. Grace, theologically speaking, refers to the love of God that spills over into creation and into our lives. Grace assures us that we are favored by a God who is totally "for us." It points to the proximate Presence of a God, whom St. Catherine of Siena, the fourteenth-century mystic, addressed as "O mad lover… because you have fallen in love with what you have created.… You clothed yourself in our humanity, and nearer than that you could not have come."[15]

Traces of grace glimmer throughout human life, because divine Love was made flesh and dwells among us. The mystery of the Incarnation celebrates the reality that God was not satisfied with loving us from afar, but drew near to love us close by. Grace or the loving approach of God into our lives is draped in matter and made manifest in the concrete people and events of our ordinary lives. Indeed, God gives us God's very self in creation. Ignatian spirituality embraces the goodness of all created reality as well as the goodness of God, who is its Source and Destiny. Contrary to earth-depreciating spiritualities that denigrate the things of this life in favor of the blessings to be enjoyed in the life to come, Ignatian spirituality is earth-affirming.[16] It invites us to perceive all that exists as genuine gifts from God to be enjoyed insofar as they contribute to lives of love now and into eternity. By moving us to embrace the goodness of all created reality, our appreciation and esteem of creation are true doorways to gratitude. Gratitude was so prized by Ignatius, because he saw it as the threshold to love of God, from whom all blessings flow. Our gratitude span expands to the extent that we recognize and appreciate grace moments that glimmer through the day and signal the active presence of God.

God's Presence in Both Light and Darkness

In our search for God's presence in our life, we naturally turn to positive experiences of peace and love, wonder and joy. We identify "God moments" as times of consolation, when we experience God's love and feel an ability to trust God in all aspects of our life. It is easy for us to spot the presence of God in these positive experiences of light. While affirming these moments as tangible experiences of God's self-communication to us, Rahner also directs our attention to difficult and dark times. He suggests that God can often be experienced at times in life, when "everyday realities break and dissolve," when we struggle with meaning at work, betrayal in relationships, dryness in prayer, and disillusionment with authority.[17] At such times, we may experience the divine Presence as a surprising ability to endure and to hope in the face of hardship and opposition. In some unfathomable way, we discover a Source of strength that goes beyond anything we can attribute to ourselves. Rahner points to this sustaining Source as the mysterious presence of the God of Light, upholding us in our dark night.

In an excerpted piece from her book, published in *Lumunos: Faith & Light for the Journey*, Becky Garrison recounts her experience of this God of Darkness. Fittingly, the piece is entitled, "Where is God?" Growing up with alcoholic parents, she describes her painful childhood.

> Over time my parents slowly started to lose little pieces of themselves. As they got worse, the shame of my family's demise drove my extended family and all their friends to seek higher ground, leaving us black sheep to forage for ourselves. Bit by bit they started to go. I

don't know at what point my parents' souls actually left their bodies, after which, I pray, they were welcomed into God's loving arms. But it was pretty clear that by the time we buried them, there was nothing left.[18]

Struggling with the darkness of her dysfunctional childhood, she anguished over God's inscrutable ways: "Why did God seem to take a dirt nap as I buried my father and mother within an eleven-month period? This isn't how a sixteen-year-old's life is supposed to go." In an attempt to console her and her siblings, the priest who officiated at her father's funeral reassured them, recounting how much good their father had done for so many. "Even though your father couldn't help himself, he was there for countless others who were lost," he told them. "I've been getting calls for hours from people saying how much the Reverend Dr. Karl Claudius Garrison Jr. changed their lives," he added. Then at the funeral, he reminded them of the "obligation to keep on living and loving, loving and dying." At the time, the priest's words provided not "one lick of spiritual solace." Yet, those words stuck with her and made her wonder if God's light had not mysteriously slipped into her dark experiences.

> …the words by some priest I only met once and didn't care for one whit (mild understatement) said something that enabled me to hang on to life like some demented, rabid pit bull. In hindsight, I can see the hand of God working through this unknown priest and a few other kind souls. Their words entered into me like tiny specks of sunlight, illuminating what otherwise was a dark, cavernous pit that stank to high heaven.[19]

"For reasons I cannot explain," she shares, "my teenage blues never morphed into clinical depression or worse. I survived the loss of a close friend who committed suicide during my senior year of college...." Garrison's story attests to the truth of Rahner's insight that God is in the darkness, as well as in the light.

AN IGNATIAN WAY OF FINDING GOD IN ALL THINGS

We will be helped greatly to find God in all our experiences, especially negative ones, if we always keep in mind that faith is not our way to God on our terms, but God's way to us on God's terms.[20] As we described in chapter two, this conviction of the mysterious approach of God into each of our lives made Bill Spohn's experience of dying one of consolation, a peace beyond all understanding. As a person formed by the Spiritual Exercises of St. Ignatius, Bill was trained to spot the traces of grace everywhere. Jesuit Howard Gray, a contemporary interpreter of Ignatian spirituality, presents the Ignatian method of detecting God's presence as a threefold process of attention, reverence, and devotion.

> First, bring focus to your life by taking the time to listen to others and to see what lies before you. Bring yourself to a self-possession before reality. Then give your attention (maybe attentiveness is a better word) to what is really there. For example, let that person or that poem or that social injustice or that scientific experiment become as genuinely itself as it can be. Then reverence what you see before you. Reverence is giving acceptance to, cherishing the differences of, holding in awe the uniqueness of another reality. So, before you judge or assess or respond, give yourself time to esteem and accept what is there in the other. And if you learn to do this, Ignatius urged, then you will gradually discover devotion, the singularly moving

way in which God works in that situation, revealing goodness and fragility, beauty and truth, pain and anguish, wisdom and ingenuity.[21]

Attention: Fostering an attentive awareness is the first step in the Ignatian method of discovering the presence and action of God in our experience. This stance consists in what Jesuit theologian Walter Burghardt terms "contemplation" or "a long and loving look at the real."[22] Burghardt understands the *real* in concrete terms: as "living, pulsing people," as "fire and ice," as "the sun setting over the Swiss Alps, a gentle doe streaking through the forest," as "a ruddy glass of Burgundy," as "a child lapping a chocolate ice-cream cone" and as "a striding woman with wind-blown hair." Contemplation entails a long and loving look at such realities.

Contemplation requires *looking* at reality without analyzing or arguing with it, without describing or defining it. To contemplate, states Burghardt, is to have an encounter with the real in which "I am one with it. I do not move around it; I enter into it. Lounging by a stream, I do not exclaim, "Ah, H_2O!" I let the water trickle gently through my fingers."

Contemplation requires a *long* look at the real. According to Burghardt, the look is neither pressured nor measured by clock time, "but wonderfully unhurried, gloriously unhurried." Contemplation is resting in the real, not lifelessly or languidly, but in a way that is "alive" and "incredibly responsive, vibrating to every throb of the real." In contrast to "an endless line of tourists, ten seconds each without ever stopping," contemplation is more like "a lone young man at rest on a stone bench, eyes riveted, whole person enraptured, sensible only of beauty and mystery, aware only of the real."

Finally, the long look that contemplation involves is a *loving* one. Neither a fixed stare nor "the long look of a Judas," contemplation is being enthralled, captivated by sparkling beauty and delightful being. If contemplation means pausing long enough to notice the wondrous gifts of creation, then it is easy to appreciate Shug's comment in Alice Walker's *The Color Purple* that "it pisses God off when we walk by the color purple in a field somewhere and don't notice it." Attention, in the Ignatian method, entails cultivating a contemplative gaze in daily life.

A commitment to attentive living does not require that we leave home in search of a mountain or desert hideaway where we can dwell in seclusion and uninterrupted meditation. Rather, a contemplative attitude challenges us to take in our existing reality with spiritually sensitive eyes. Anthony de Mello recounts an instructive exchange between a disciple and a spiritual master that highlights the importance of looking carefully at everything that surrounds us in order to discover God's presence everywhere.[23]

> The disciple began the conversation: "For years" he said, "I have been seeking God. I have sought him everywhere that he is said to be: on mountain peaks, the vastness of the desert, the silence of the cloister, and the dwellings of the poor."
>
> In reply, the master asked: "Have you found him?"
>
> "No. I have not," answered the disciple. "Have you?"
>
> What could the master say? The evening sun was sending shafts of golden light into the room. Hundreds of sparrows were twittering on a nearby banyan tree. In the distance one could hear the sound of highway traffic.
>
> A mosquito droned a warning that it was going to strike....
>
> And yet this man could sit there and say he had not found God.
>
> After a while the disappointed disciple left to search elsewhere.

Another de Mello story about "The Little Fish" nicely encapsulates the wisdom of the spiritual master:

"Excuse me," said an ocean fish.
"You are older than I, so
can you tell me where to find
this thing they call the ocean?"

"The ocean," said the older fish,
"is the thing you are in now."

"Oh, this? But this is water.
What I'm seeking is the ocean,"
said the disappointed fish,
as he swam away to search elsewhere.

The spiritual lesson to us is clear: "There isn't anything to look *for*. All you have to do is *look*."[24]

Too often the fast pace of life detracts from this kind of contemplative attention. Rushing robs us of the ability to appreciate the experiences that fill our day. That is why the Ignatian method emphasizes the importance of "staying with." Staying with present experience can enhance enjoyment and pleasure, but it can also deepen discomfort and pain. This is probably why we spend so little time dwelling in the present and so much time in fantasy and speculation. As psychoanalyst Claudio Naranjo puts it, "The experience of doing nothing but attending to the contents of awareness may lead…to a self-rewarding contact with reality, or to intense discomfort. When left with nothing but the obvious, our attitude towards ourselves and towards our existence becomes apparent. Particularly so, the negatives ones."[25] Staying with the present requires accepting our immediate experience and being alert to how we can heed the command of God to choose life (Deut 30:19) in the midst of what we are going through.

Aware of the danger of rushing and missing the depth and significance of our experiences, Ignatius advises those making the Spiritual Exercises to take their time and to savor their meditations, "For it is not much knowledge that fills and satisfies the soul, but the intimate understanding and relish of the truth."[26] He warns against anticipating the future in such a way that distracts from the present.[27] And when giving instructions about praying over a traditional prayer, he states, "If in contemplation, say on the Our Father, he [she] finds in one or two words abundant matter for thought and much relish and consolation, he [she] should not be anxious to go on, though the whole hour be taken up with what he [she] had found."[28] Finally, Ignatius stresses the importance of "staying with" in his directive that retreatants pray over the same topic or mystery of the gospel at least twice. In these periods of prayer called the "repetition," he states that "attention should be given to some more important parts in which one has experienced understanding, consolation, or desolation."[29] The repetition enables the retreatant to return to places in a past prayer period where something important was going on, as indicated by an exciting illumination or intense feelings of consolation or desolation. The return is for the purpose of deepening the movement of grace in one's life.

Reverence. The second movement of the Ignatian method for finding God in all things calls for respecting the unique "otherness" of everything that surrounds us. People, especially, are to be regarded as unprecedented selves. It requires being fresh in our perception, not being distracted by preoccupations and prejudices. Priest-psychologist Stephen Rossetti describes how challenging it is to regard others with the freshness that reverence requires.

We do not always "see" the people around us, especially if they are well known to us. We have set in cement our ideas about these familiar faces and we tend to filter out any information that contradicts it. The patterns are set. And thus we do not give others a chance to change or to surprise us.

Could we try, this day, to see those familiar faces around us with a mind free of old labels? Could we let go of the mental constraints we place on others? If we are able to do so, maybe those closest to us will surprise us. They may even amaze us. Perhaps Jesus is still among us, present in others, but we fail to recognize him.[30]

Calling for an undefended and unguarded openness, reverence entails a certain vulnerability that lets persons and events impact us with their full resonance. Reverence excludes any kind of attempt to manipulate, control, or categorize people, but to allow them to speak for themselves, to express their meaning and truth in their own words. In the language of spiritual direction, reverence is the heart of contemplative listening. Eugene Peterson, a Presbyterian pastor and author, captures the nature of a reverential stance in describing the life of faith:

> The life of faith does not consist in imposing our will (or God's will!) either on other persons or on the material world around us. Instead of making the world around us or the people around us or our own selves into the image of what we think is good, we enter the lifelong process of no longer arranging the world and the people on our terms. We embrace what is given to us—people, spouse, children, forests, weather, city—just as they are given to us, and sit and stare, look and listen until we begin to see and hear

the God-dimensions in each gift, and engage with what God has given, with what he [sic] is doing.[31]

In short, the attention and reverence called for by the Ignatian method resemble the spirit of *lectio divina,* an ancient prayer form that involves reading a biblical text in a way that allows it to address us in a personal and heartfelt way. In the Ignatian method, however, the sacred text consists in the totality of our life experience.

Embedded in our concrete experiences is the graceful communication of God. Like Moses before the burning bush, we need to approach the events of ordinary life with our shoes off, recognizing that our experiences too are holy ground because they are pregnant with the presence of God. With the eyes of faith, every common bush can be revelatory of God. As Elizabeth Barrett Browning proclaims, "Earth's crammed with heaven, / And every common bush afire with God. / But only he who sees, takes off his shoes. / The rest sit round it and pluck blackberries...."[32] Jesuit Charles O'Neill, however, muses insightfully that the converse of Browning's insight is also an important truth: "He is helped to see, who takes off his shoes."[33] So reverence is not only a response to encountering the divine Mystery, but also an important precondition for "seeing" God in the ordinary. In either case, a reverent posture primes us for an encounter with the living God and an experience of devotion.

Devotion: Finally, devotion in the Ignatian method celebrates the gift of God's ongoing self-disclosure in the context of ordinary life. Ignatius believed firmly that God deals directly and intimately with each of us (*Spiritual Exercises,* no. 15). God does this by touching us in our interior experiences of remembering, understanding, and desiring. Thus, he encouraged people who are seeking God's guidance to hold their question with openness in their hearts, trusting that God will, in God's time, bring them to some clarity regarding how best to proceed. God will provide this guidance by illuminating their minds with a telling insight or by stirring their hearts with a recurrent deep desire to move in a certain direction.

To detect God's presence and lead, however, requires that we stay with things until the veil drops, allowing reality to be revelatory. Often we do not linger long enough to get the message. Rabbi Lawrence Kushner emphasizes the importance of staying with things patiently, in order to discern God's presence and voice in the often-perplexing realities of our life. To bring this point home, he offers a humorous deconstruction of Moses' experience before the burning bush, suggesting that what occurred there was not so much a miracle, but a test of Moses' capacity to pay attention. "The story is customarily offered as 'miracle' that God performed to get Moses' attention," Kushner explains. "This fails to explain why God, who could split the sea, fashion pillars of fire, and make the sun stand still would resort to something as trivial and undramatic as to make a bush burn without being consumed to attract Moses' attention."[34] He notes that in the process of combustion, even dry kindling wood takes several minutes before it is burned up. So, for Moses to "get" what was occurring before his very eyes, he had to have looked at the bush for at least several minutes. If he had just given it a passing glance, he would not have noticed the miracle. Thus, Kushner concludes, "The 'burning bush' was not a miracle. It was a test. God wanted to find out whether or not Moses could pay attention to something for more than a few minutes. When Moses did, God spoke."[35] Many of us often miss the self-disclosures of God in the midst of our busy lives, because we fail to stay attentive long enough "to get it." "The trick," Kushner concludes "is to pay attention to what is going on around you long enough to behold the miracle without falling asleep. There is another world, right here within this one, whenever we pay attention."[36] Despite the importance of staying awake so as not to miss God's disclosure to us, the paradox is that God's supportive guidance is also given to us when we are asleep, in our dreams.

Such was the experience of Jacob at a perplexing and troubling time in his life. "Surely the LORD is in this place—and I did not know it!" These words burst from Jacob's lips as he woke from a dream-filled sleep (Gen 28:16). Overnight, he felt his situation change dramatically. In a vivid dream that flooded him with fresh hope, he heard God say to him in so many words: "Jacob, you don't have to worry; everything is still right between us. I will continue to honor the covenant I have with you and bless you with land and posterity. Be assured that I am with you and will keep you safe wherever you go; I will never desert you nor fail to come through for you as I promised." What a reassuring message for Jacob, caught in the middle of a family crisis that he had brought upon himself by robbing his older brother Esau of the blessing that rightfully belonged to the firstborn. Already, he was paying for what he had done—having to leave home in a hurry to escape Esau's avenging rage. Fortunately, Rebekah, his quick-thinking mother, came to his rescue and sent him off to find refuge with her family in a far-off land. Safe for the moment, Jacob was still left with fears about his uncertain future. So the dream's message brought much relief to him as he struggled to deal with the sudden turmoil in his life. He had the strength to keep going because he believed that even in this crisis God was present. "How awesome is this place! This is none other than the house of God, and this is the gate of heaven" (Gen 28:17).

Among the various gospel accounts of the sower and the seed, one is often unnoticed because of its brevity. In four short verses, Mark relates the story of a man who scatters seed on the land. Night and day, while he is asleep or awake, the seed is sprouting and growing; he does not know how. On its own, the earth produces first the shoot, then the ear, then the full grain in the ear. When the crop is ripe, the sower at once starts to reap because the harvest has come (Mark 4:26–29), This parable conveys Jesus' teaching that our God is a God of light and a God of darkness, who supports us in our journey "night and day," while we are awake and while we are asleep.

Ignatian devotion stems from the conviction that reality, when regarded with reverence and wonder, alludes to something beyond itself. It is this allusion that conveys to us "the awareness of a spiritual dimension of reality, the relatedness of being to transcendent meaning."[37] Perceiving creation with reverence and marvel leads to awe—a sense for the reference everywhere to God who is beyond all creating things. Reverence enables us to perceive intimations of the divine in the midst of daily life. When we regard reality with reverent awe, we open ourselves to receiving "an answer of the heart and mind to the presence of mystery in all things, *an intuition for a meaning that is beyond the mystery,* an awareness of the transcendent worth of the universe."[38] In describing the revelation that comes through reverent wonder, Rabbi Abraham Heschel states, "True, the mystery of meaning is silent. There is no speech, there are no words, the voice is not heard. Yet beyond our reasoning and beyond our believing there is a *preconceptual* faculty that senses the glory, the presence of the Divine. We do not perceive it. We have no knowledge; we only have awareness. We witness it."[39] The Ignatian method invites us to enter reverently into the garden of creation and there to witness the presence of God, who at every moment sustains us and all things in existence.

Ignatius perceived the world as a divine milieu in which God is everywhere to be found. The following story delightfully portrays this view of a God-soaked world:

> God decided to become visible to a king and a peasant and sent an angel to inform them of the blessed event. "O king," the angel announced. "God has deigned to

be revealed to you in whatever manner you wish. In what form do you want God to appear?"

Seated pompously on his throne and surrounded by awestruck subjects, the king royally proclaimed: "How else would I wish to see God, save in majesty and power? Show God to us in the full glory of power."

God granted his wish and appeared as a bolt of lightning that instantly pulverized the king and his court. Nothing, not even a cinder, remained.

The angel then manifested herself to a peasant saying: "God deigns to be revealed to you in whatever manner you desire. How do you wish to see God?"

Scratching his head and puzzling a long while, the peasant finally said: "I am a poor man and not worthy to see God face to face. But if it is God's will to be revealed to me, let it be in those things with which I am familiar. Let me see God in the earth I plough, the water I drink, and the food I eat. Let me see the presence of God in the faces of my family, neighbors, and—if God deems it as good for myself and others— even in my own reflection as well."[40]

The Ignatian method of attention, reverence, and devotion facilitates our ability to find God in all things.

GRATITUDE AND THE GOOD NEWS

Jesus' principal message throughout his public ministry was straightforward: The reign of God is here. God's loving power is available as support for living an abundant life. Belief that the reign of God is in our midst should alter our way of looking at all our experiences. It can serve as a window through which we can better spot gratitude-evoking events in daily life. The presence of God in our world remains God's gift. To bind the mystery of God into a distant and inaccessible realm robs us of experiencing the sacredness of everyday and the abundance of gifts that make life a blessing. Deists, who believe in a distant God, are not alone in ruling out the experience of God's gracious presence in life. Those who believe that religious experience is restricted just to those who are "religious" or "pious" are also guilty. Theologian Nicholas Lash warns of the danger of setting up a "'God-district' alongside the other districts" in our life, "and, by so doing, to obscure the signs of God's address and presence both in that district and elsewhere."[41] Arguing that the experience of God is not something other than the general experiences had in ordinary life, Lash states, "It is easy to get stuck in the world of religion and having done so, to fail to find one's way back to the hearing of God's address and the celebration of his presence in all the ordinary places and problems of our world."[42] To support his argument, Lash recounts an experience of the Jewish philosopher, Martin Buber.

> "In my earlier years," he [Buber] tells us, "'religious experience' was the experience of an otherness which did not fit into the context of life." Then one day, "after a morning of 'religious' enthusiasm, I had a visit from an unknown young man, without being there in spirit. I certainly did not fail to let the meeting be friendly," but "omitted to guess the question which he did not put." Shortly afterwards, he heard of the young man's death. Since that day [Buber said], "I possess nothing but the everyday out which I am never taken...."[43]

Living everyday centered on the present way is key to discovering God's gracious presence in the ordinary. Strongly influenced by this experience, Buber believed that "a God who is sought, or celebrated, or obeyed *elsewhere* than in the everyday (in religion, for example) is a figment of our imagination destructive of our common humanity—and thereby destructive of our relations with God."[44] As with Moses' experience before the burning bush, all our experiences can function as a word of revelation, if we are open to listen and to see. Our ordinary life experience provides the context for living with gratefulness, for it is there that we can spot divine self-giving and the presence of God.

SPIRITUAL EXERCISES AND PERSONAL REFLECTIONS

A Parable to Encourage the Practice of Awareness

> Once a monk went to his master, complaining about the daily practices required of him to expand his capacity to be aware, to be mindful.
>
> "What has all this to do with enlightenment?" the young disciple cried out. "Will it help me become enlightened?"
>
> "What you do will have as much effect on your enlightenment as it does on the sun rising," replied the master.
>
> "Then why bother?" asked the young monk.
>
> "Ah," came the reply, "so that you will be awake when the sun does rise."[45]

God is not more present during times when we use contemplative practices to expand our awareness. Rather, it is *we* who are more present to the ever-present God in our daily lives.

Practicing Being Present-Centered

Sit quietly and take some time to be attentive to your present experience, from moment to moment. Just be an observer of your awareness and notice where it goes.

Follow the spontaneous flow of your awareness. Say to yourself, "Right now I'm aware of..." and complete this sentence with whatever you are aware of at the moment.

Continue to report what you are aware of from moment to moment for about ten minutes.

What are you aware of in terms of your:

- bodily sensations (e.g., tightness in your stomach? tension in your neck? a backache?)

- feelings/emotions (e.g., anxious? sad? peaceful?)

- perceptions (what are you seeing, hearing, touching, smelling?)

- mental activities (e.g., thoughts, worries, concerns, hopes, fantasies)

For example:

- "Right now, I'm aware of feeling excited about describing this exercise."

- "Right now, I'm aware of a slight tension in the small of my back."

- "Right now, I'm wondering how comfortable you'll be with experimenting with this practice of awareness."

- "Right now, I'm imagining that some of you will find this to be a quick way of centering yourself and focusing on the present."

As the Creator of the Universe reminded Moses as he stood before the burning bush: "...the place on which you are standing is holy ground" (Exod 3:5). The "right now" of our lives is holy ground because it is where God is to be encountered.

Epilogue

❧

"FOR ALL THAT HAS BEEN, THANKS. For all that will be, yes." These words of the late Secretary General of the United Nations, Dag Hammarskjöld, sum up the spirituality of gratitude expressed in this book. In the end, a spiritual path is most Christian when it leads to a gratefulness for all that is and has been, and a trusting surrender to God for all that will be in the unfolding mystery of our life. Gratefulness is a vision of reality—all that we are and have are gifts from a good and giving God, in whom "we live and move and have our being" (Acts 17:28). Gratitude is the spiritual practice that enables us to wholeheartedly trust in God's abiding faithfulness.

Gratitude and trust clearly marked the life of Jesus. His prayer just before calling forth his friend Lazarus from the tomb captured his over-all gratitude to God: "Father, I thank you for having heard me. I knew that you always hear me, but I have said this for the sake of the crowd standing here, so that they may believe that you sent me" (John 11:41–42). And it was his faith and trust in the reliability of God that allowed him to pray on the cross, "Father, into your hands, I commend my spirit" (Luke 23:46).

Gratitude is the echo of grace. Whenever we recognize that we have been touched by grace, our hearts spontaneously resound with gratitude. That grace already abounds richly in all our lives is the central motif of this book, and with this belief, we have focused on how to open our eyes to this vision of reality. We have offered examples of scriptural lenses that can help us catch the rhyme between biblical events and our own experiences, because it is when we see the analogy between biblical stories and our own lives that we come to understand that Scripture is not just an account of what God has done in the past, but what God is always doing. In this way, Scripture can help expand our awareness of the ongoing activity of God on our behalf today. We have also suggested that the *Spiritual Exercises of Ignatius of Loyola* can be a valuable resource for enhancing our gratitude, because it focuses our attention on God's gracious love, manifested in multiple ways: in the creation of the world and the gift of our own life, as well as in the life, death, and resurrection of Jesus. Truly, "From [God's] fullness we have all received, grace upon grace" (John 1:16). Recognizing that we are recipients of such divine generosity paves the way to grateful living. As a contemporary spiritual writer clearly expresses:

> When we are…able to accept being accepted, able to receive the loving, listening presence of God both embodied in others and hidden in their hearts, we experience God as love. The experience of such love results spontaneously in gratitude, praise, and joy. This is not the "duty of being grateful" I'm speaking of. I mean an upwelling of heart-breaking, heart-opening thankfulness, and joy that such love could be, that we could be in it, that it could be in us, that we are all in it together.[1]

It is no wonder, then, that Christians through the centuries have joined together in worship, singing with joyful thanksgiving:

Now thank we all our God
with heart and hands and voices;
Who wondrous things have done,
in Whom this world rejoices.
Who from our mother's arms,
Has blessed us on our way,
With countless gifts of love,

And still is ours today.

—Martin Rinkart (c.1636)

Notes

INTRODUCTION

1. Kim Rosen, *Saved by a Poem* (Carlsbad, CA: Hay House, 2009), quoted by Valerie Anderson, *Los Angeles Times*, November 22, 2009.

2. Patricia Livingston, "Slipping into the Arms of Love," *Living Faith*, May 28, 2006.

3. Dorothy Foltz-Gray, "What Really Makes Us Happy," *Prevention*, February 2006, 156.

4. Ibid.

5. Quoted in Robert A. Emmons, *Thanks! How the New Science of Gratitude Can Make You Happier* (Boston: Houghton Mifflin, 2007), 7.

6. Aristotle, *Nicomachean Ethics*, trans. D. Ross, rev. J. L. Ackrill and J. O. Urmson (Oxford: Oxford University Press, 1980), bk. 4, 92.

7. Lloyd Geering, "A Ecological Faith for the Global Era," *Ecotheology* 6.1/6.2 (July 2001): 20.

8. Sam Keen, *Apology for Wonder* (New York: Harper and Row, 1969), 34.

9. Ibid., 35.

10. Abraham J. Heschel, *God in Search of Man: A Philosophy of Judaism* (New York: Harper and Row, 1955), 108.

11. Larry James Peacock, *Openings: A Daybook of Saints, Psalms, and Prayer* (Nashville: Upper Room Books, 2003), 208.

12. Peter Schineller, "St. Ignatius and Creation-Centered Spirituality," *The Way* 29, no. 1 (January 1989): 50.

13. Ibid. 51.

14. Kathleen Fischer, *Loving Creation: Christian Spirituality, Earth-Centered and Just* (New York/Mahwah, NJ: Paulist Press, 2009), 136.

15. Ibid., 137.

16. Drew Christiansen, "Christian Theology and Ecological Responsibility," *America*, May 23, 1992, 450.

17. *Spiritual Exercises*, no. 234.

18. Dietrich Bonhoeffer, *Letters and Papers from Prison*, ed. E. Bethge (New York: Macmillan, 1967), 370.

19. Rufus Jones, quoted in Catherine Whitmire, *Plain Living: A Quaker Path to Simplicity* (Notre Dame, IN: Sorin Books, 2002), 127.

20. Bella Brown, quoted in Whitmire, *Plain Living*, 67.

CHAPTER 1

1. G. K. Chesterton, *St. Francis of Assisi* (1924; repr., New York: Doubleday, 1990), 78.

2. Robert A. Emmons and Michael E. McCullough, "Counting Blessings versus Burdens: An Experimental Investigation of Gratitude and Subjective Well-Being in Daily Life," *Journal of Personality and Social Psychology* 84, no. 2 (2003): 377–389.

3. Michael E. McCullough, Robert A. Emmons, and Jo-Ann Tsang, "The Grateful Disposition: A Conceptual and Empirical Topography," *Journal of Personality and Social Psychology* 82, no. 1 (2002): 112–127.

4. Ibid., 112.

5. Ibid., 113.

6. Giacomo Bono, Robert A. Emmons, and Michael E. McCullough, "Gratitude in Practice and the Practice of Gratitude," in *Positive Psychology in Practice*, ed. P. Alex Linley and Stephen Joseph (Hoboken, NJ: Wiley, 2004), 469.

7. Jennifer R. Dunn and Maurice E. Schweitzer, "Feeling and Believing: The Influence of Emotion on Trust," *Journal of Personality and Social Psychology* 88, no. 5 (2005): 745.

8. Adapted from Anthony de Mello, SJ, *Sadhana: A Way to God* (St. Louis: Institute of Jesuit Sources, 1978), 86–87.

9. Julian of Norwich, *The Revelations of Divine Love*, chap. 5, quoted in Jeffrey D. Imbach, *The Recovery of Love: Christian Mysticism and the Addictive Society* (New York: Crossroad, 1992), 51.

10. Ibid.

11. Kyung M. Song, "Researchers Explore the How and Why of Happiness," *Seattle Times*, February 12, 2004.

12. Robert A. Emmons, *Thanks! How the New Science of Gratitude Can Make You Happier* (Boston: Houghton Mifflin, 2007), 23.

13. Ibid., 24.

14. Ibid., 24–25.

15. Bono, Emmons, and McCullough, 473–474.

16. Seward Hiltner, *Theological Dynamics* (New York: Abingdon, 1972), 46–47.

17. Ibid., 47.

18. Uwe E. Reinhardt, "The Trouble with U.S. Military Medicine," *British Medical Journal* 334 (March 17, 2007): 565.

19. Robert C. Roberts, "The Blessings of Gratitude: A Conceptual Analysis," in *The Psychology of Gratitude*, ed. Robert A. Emmons and Michael E. McCullough (New York: Oxford University Press, 2004), 61.

20. Roy F. Baumeister and Stacey A. Ilko, "Shallow Gratitude: Public and Private Acknowledgement of External

Help in Accounts of Success," *Basic and Applied Social Psychology* 16, nos. 1 and 2 (1995): 191–209.

21. Roberts, "Blessings of Gratitude," 60–61.

22. Bono, Emmons, and McCullough, 477 (emphasis added).

23. Dorothy Foltz-Gray, "What Really Makes Us Happy," *Prevention*, February 2006, 156–163.

24. Anthony de Mello, SJ, *One-Minute Wisdom* (Garden City, NY: Doubleday, 1985), 24–25.

25. David Steindl-Rast, "Gratitude as Thankfulness and as Gratefulness," in *The Psychology of Gratitude*, ed. Emmons and McCullough, 286.

26. Ibid.

27. David Steindl-Rast quoted in Patricia Lefevere, "Spirituality of Gratefulness Begins with Existential 'Wow!' at God's Giving," *National Catholic Reporter*, December 8, 2000.

28. Steindl-Rast, "Gratitude as Thankfulness," 287.

29. Ibid.

30. Ibid., 286.

31. Douglas V. Steere, quoted in Catherine Whitmire, *Plain Living: A Quaker Path to Simplicity* (Notre Dame, IN: Sorin Books, 2001), 68.

32. Bernard Berenson, quoted in William Barry, SJ, *Finding God in All Things* (Notre Dame, IN: Ave Maria Press, 1995), 35.

33. Robert Byrd, quoted in Barry, *Finding God in All Things*, 35.

34. Abraham Maslow, quoted in Steindl-Rast, "Gratitude as Thankfulness," 289.

35. Ibid.

36. Ibid., 288.

37. Quoted in Emmons, *Thanks! How the New Science of Gratitude Can Make You Happier*, 195.

CHAPTER 2

1. James and Evelyn Whitehead, *Holy Eros: Recovering the Passion of God* (Maryknoll, NY: Orbis, 2009), 177.

2. Quoted in Martha E. Stortz, "The School of Hope," *Santa Clara*, Winter 2006.

3. Ibid.

4. Ibid.

5. Ibid.

6. Ibid.

7. Ibid.

8. Ibid.

9. Standard practice when referring to the text of the *Spiritual Exercises* is to italicize the title and not italicize the terms when referring to it as a retreat experience.

10. Quoted in Martha E. Stortz, "Follow the Friendships: The Work of William Spohn," *Explore* (Spring 2007), 8.

11. John C. Olin, introduction to *The Autobiography of St. Ignatius with Related Documents*, trans. Joseph F. O'Callaghan (New York: Harper and Row, 1974), 12.

12. Peter Schineller, "St. Ignatius and Creation-Centered Spirituality," *The Way* 29, no. 1 (January 1989): 50.

13. For a full textual argument in support of gratitude as a leitmotif of the entire *Spiritual Exercises*, see Wilkie Au, "Ignatian Service: Gratitude and Love in Action," *Studies in the Spirituality of Jesuits* 40, no. 2 (Summer 2008).

14. *Spiritual Exercises*, nos. 230–237.

15. Ibid., no. 233.

16. Ibid., nos. 233, 234, 237.

17. This threefold Ignatian dynamic is reflected in Gospel accounts describing the ministerial outreach of Jesus. "Perceiving," "seeing" was the beginning of the compassionate actions of Jesus. For example, once a leper approached Jesus, begging to be cured (Mark 1:40–45). Jesus takes in the reality

of this afflicted suppliant, paying close attention to his words and actions. Then, moved with compassion, he reaches out to touch the diseased person. Jesus' therapeutic touch issued forth from a compassionate heart. This episode exemplifies a three-fold dynamic that characterizes many of Jesus' healing encounters (e.g., Luke 7:13–14; Luke 13:10–13; Mark 6:34–35). (1) Jesus is keenly aware of his interpersonal environment, sensitive to the needs of the people around him (*contemplative perception*); (2) he lets what he perceives stir him to compassion (*affective arousal*); (3) moved by compassion, he reaches out to help (*altruistic action*).

18. Quoted in Stortz, " School of Hope."

19. Ibid.

20. Jessica Powers, "The Masses," quoted in Robert F. Morneau, *Ashes to Easter: Lenten Meditations* (New York: Crossroad, 1997), 18.

21. Katherine Dyckman, Mary Garvin, and Elizabeth Liebert, *The Spiritual Exercises Reclaimed: Uncovering Liberating Possibilities for Woman* (Mahwah, NJ: Paulist Press, 2001), 100.

22. Wendy Farley, *The Wounding and Healing of Desire: Weaving Heaven and Earth* (Louisville, KY: Westminster John Knox, 2005), 2.

23. Quoted in Stortz, "School of Hope."

24. Farley, 29.

25. William C. Spohn, *Go and Do Likewise: Jesus and Ethics* (New York: Continuum, 1999), 102–103.

26. Stortz, "School of Hope."

27. In Ignatian spirituality, service takes on great significance because it is seen as a way of collaborating with God. In this joint effort, we are most united to Christ when our actions issue forth from "a pure intention of the divine service." Thus, Ignatius encourages an ongoing purification of our motives for serving others. While human action generally arises from many levels of motivation—conscious and unconscious—the ideal is

that our works of service, compassion, and justice originate more and more from feelings of gratitude and love, rather than from deficient motives such as fear of punishment, desire for reward, self-aggrandizement, guilt, and compulsion. Therefore, our commitment to service must, as Jesuit John J. English states, "take place in the context of God's goodness…forgiving love… concern for [humankind] and the support [God] gives to persons who desire social justice and peace." As we mentioned above, the basic dynamic by which Ignatius leads people to a commitment to service originates with gratitude. In sum, affective awareness of God's gracious love generates gratitude, which, for Ignatius, serves as a springboard to loving service. Even though all that we possess has been given to us by God, nothing is required of us in return. Genuine love never demands reciprocation. We do not owe God anything. Nevertheless, love urges us on to an intimate mutuality with a God who loves us so abundantly. As Jesuit William Meissner rightly observes of Ignatius, "Motifs of love and service are thus fused into a common and mutually sustaining theme pervading all of his spirituality." In short, through the *Spiritual Exercises*, Ignatius hopes to form people who are open to being touched by God in a way that illumines their perception of God's presence and action, stirs their heart with gratitude and love, and motivates them to assist others. Cf. Wilkie Au, "Ignatian Service: Gratitude and Love in Action," *Studies in the Spirituality of Jesuits* 40, no. 2 (Summer 2008): 3–4, 13.

28. Anne E. Patrick, SNJM, "Jesus and the Moral Life: Edwards, H. R. Niebuhr, and Spohn," *Explore* (Spring 2007): 14.

29. Quoted in Stortz, "School of Hope."

30. William C. Spohn, "The Chosen Path," *America*, July 21–28, 2003, 12.

31. *Spiritual Exercises*, no. 230.

32. Philip C. Watkins, Jason Scheer, Melinda Ovnicek, and Russell Kolts, "The Debt of Gratitude: Disassociating Gratitude and Indebtedness," *Cognition and Emotion* 20, no. 2 (2006): 236.

33. Quoted in Robert A. Emmons and Teresa T. Kneezel, "Giving Thanks: Spiritual and Religious Correlates of Gratitude," *Journal of Psychology and Christianity* 24, no. 2 (2005): 140.

34. *Letters of St. Ignatius of Loyola*, trans. and ed. William J. Young (Chicago: Loyola University Press, 1959), 55, quoted in Schineller, "St. Ignatius and Creation-Centered Spirituality," 50.

35. *Spiritual Exercises*, no. 48, regarding the Second Prelude. Jesuit Edward Kinerk makes a perceptive observation about how Ignatius' instructing retreatants to pray for particular graces involved a kind of "schooling of desires." He states,

> In this age of personalism, one of the more startling aspects of the *Spiritual Exercises* is the final prelude to each meditation. Here Ignatius tells the retreatant the particular grace which should be asked for, "that which I want and desire." How, one might well ask, can I ask for something that I may not really want? Should my desires not be more spontaneous and above all personal? Should I not be asking for what *I* want and desire instead of for what *Ignatius* tells me to want and desire?

In response to this criticism, Kinerk suggests

> ...that Ignatius is not mandating desires but eliciting them, and he does this by interesting the retreatant's imagination. Imagine yourself before Christ on the cross and ask yourself what you want to do for Christ. Imagine yourself before Christ the King and see if you do not desire to respond to his call. Imagine yourself with Christ in the Garden and see if you don't desire to experience sorrow with Christ? In effect, Ignatius is telling the retreatant, 'Try this on for size. See if it fits you and make it your own.

E. Edward Kinerk, SJ, "Eliciting Great Desires: Their Place in the Spirituality of the Society of Jesus," *Studies in the Spirituality of Jesuits* 16, no. 5 (November 1984): 9–11.

36. Anthony de Mellow, SJ, *Song of the Bird* (Garden City, NY: Doubleday, 1984), 2.

37. Stortz, "Follow the Friendships," 9.

38. Ibid.

39. *Spiritual Exercises*, no. 15.

40. Ibid., no. 2.

41. James D. Whitehead, "Priestliness: A Crisis of Belonging," in *Being a Priest Today*, ed. Donald J. Goergen (Collegeville, MN: Liturgical Press, 1992), 25.

42. Johannes B. Metz, *Poverty of Spirit*, trans. John Drury (New York: Paulist Press, 1968), 7.

CHAPTER 3

1. Ernest Kurtz and Katherine Ketcham, *The Spirituality of Imperfection: Storytelling and the Search for Meaning* (New York: Bantam, 1992), 175.

2. William James, *The Principles of Psychology* (Cambridge: Harvard University Press, 1983), 380–81.

3. Kathleen R. Fischer, *The Inner Rainbow: The Imagination in Christian Life* (New York/Mahwah, NJ: Paulist Press, 1983), 158.

4. Ibid., 158–159.

5. William Paul Young, *The Shack: Where Tragedy Confronts Eternity* (Newbury Park, CA: Windblown Media, 2007), 199.

6. William C. Spohn, *Go and Do Likewise: Jesus and Ethics* (New York: Continuum, 1999), 55–56.

7. Ibid., 56.

8. William C. Spohn, "The Biblical Theology of the Pastoral Letters and Ignatian Contemplation," *Studies in the Spirituality of American Jesuits* 17, no. 4 (1985): 8–9.

9. Walter Brueggemann, *The Message of the Psalms: A Theological Commentary* (Minneapolis: Augsburg, 1984), 9–23.

10. Wendy M. Wright, "The Long, Lithe Limbs of Hope," *Weavings: A Journal of the Christian Spiritual Life* 14, no. 6 (November/December 1999): 13.

11. Marcus J. Borg, *Jesus: Uncovering the Life, Teachings, and Relevance of a Religious Revolutionary* (New York: HarperCollins, 2008), 57–58.

12. Ibid., 58.

CHAPTER 4

1. This illustration has been adapted from an account in Solomon Schimmel, *The Seven Deadly Sins: Jewish, Christian, and Classical Reflections on Human Nature* (New York: Free Press, 1992), 56–57.

2. Joseph Naft, *The Sacred Art of Soul Making: Balance and Depth in Spiritual Practice* (Baltimore: I. F. Publishing, 2006), 93.

3. Johannes B. Metz, *Poverty of Spirit*, trans. John Drury (Mahwah, NJ: Paulist Press, 1969), 7.

4. *Diagnostic and Statistical Manual of Mental Disorders*, 4th ed. (Washington, DC: American Psychiatric Association, 1994), 658–659, 661.

5. Ibid., 659.

6. David S. Gerson quoted in Tim Rice, "New Economy Executives are Smitten, and Undone, by Their Own Images," *New York Times,* July 29, 2002.

7. Jay A. Conger quoted in Rice, "New Economy Executives."

8. Ibid.

9. Sam Vaknin quoted in Rice, "New Economy Executives."

10. Ibid.

11. Stanley Renshon quoted in Bill Dalton, "Philandering Politicians: What Makes 'Em Do It," *Prime Buzz*, June 25, 2009, http://primebuzz.kcstar.com/?q=node/19040.

12. Ibid.

13. Frank Farley, quoted in "Philandering Politicians."

14. Frank Greenstein, quoted in "Philandering Politicians."

15. Ibid.

16. Joel Stein, "The Key to iHappiness," *Los Angeles Times*, June 22, 2007.

17. Ibid.

18. Ibid.

19. Ibid.

20. Juliet B. Schor, *The Overworked American: The Unexpected Decline of Leisure* (New York: HarperCollins, 1991), 158.

21. Stein, "The Key to iHappiness."

22. Mary Jo Leddy, *Radical Gratitude* (Maryknoll, NY: Orbis, 2002), 6.

23. Ibid., 23.

24. Ibid., 40.

25. Ibid., 7.

26. Ibid.

27. Ibid., 23.

28. Ibid.

29. Philip C. Watkins, "Gratitude and Subjective Well-Being," in *The Psychology of Gratitude*, ed. Emmons and McCullough (New York: Oxford University Press, 2004), 176.

30. Leddy, 39.

31. Ibid.

32. Ibid., 29.

33. Walter Conn, *Christian Conversion: A Developmental Interpretation of Autonomy and Surrender* (Mahwah, NJ: Paulist Press, 1986), 22.

34. Ibid. 23.

35. Robert A. Johnson with Jerry M. Ruhl, *Balancing Heaven and Earth: A Memoir* (San Francisco: HarperSanFrancisco, 1998), 11.

36. Wendy Farley, *The Wounding and Healing of Desire: Weaving Heaven and Earth* (Louisville: Westminster John Knox, 2005), 12–13.

37. Ignatius of Loyola in *Hearts on Fire: Praying with Jesuits*, ed. Michael Harter, SJ (St. Louis: Institute of Jesuit Sources, 1993), 84.

38. Adapted from Robert A. Emmons, *Thanks! How the New Science of Gratitude Can Make You Happier* (Boston: Houghton Mifflin, 2007), 192–194.

39. For further information regarding the concept of the inner child, see W. Hugh Missildine, M.D., *Your Inner Child of the Past* (New York: Pocket Books, 1963), and Eric Berne, M.D., *Games People Play* (New York: Ballantine, 1964).

CHAPTER 5

1. Thomas Keating, *The Human Condition: Contemplation and Transformation* (Mahwah, NJ: Paulist Press, 1999), 21.

2. Patricia D. Nanoff, *Rising from the Dead: Stories of Women's Spiritual Journeys to Sobriety* (Binghamton, NY: Haworth Pastoral Press, 2007), 101.

3. Susan Dyke, "Getting Better Makes It Worse: Some Obstacles to Improvement in Children with Emotional and Behavioral Difficulties," *Maladjusted and Therapeutic Education* 3, no. 3, 38.

4. Ibid. 39.

5. Jim Harbaugh, SJ, *A 12-Step Approach to the Spiritual Exercises of St. Ignatius* (Franklin, WI: Sheed & Ward, 1997), 28.

6. Robert C. Roberts, "The Blessings of Gratitude: A Conceptual Analysis," in *The Psychology of Gratitude*, ed. Robert A. Emmons and Michael E. McCullough (New York: Oxford University Press, 2004), 70.

7. John Edgar Wideman, *Brothers and Keepers* (1984), quoted by Roberts, ibid.

8. Monica Furlong, "A Spirituality of Aging?" in *Reflections on Aging and Spiritual Growth*, ed. Andrew J. Weaver, Harold G. Koenig, and Phyllis C. Roe (Nashville: Abingdon, 1998), 44.

9. Ibid.

10. Phyllis C. Roe, "Turning Toward Home," in *Reflections on Aging and Spiritual Growth*, eds. Weaver, Koenig, and Roe, 69.

11. Nanoff, *Rising from the Dead*, 95.

12. Isabel Fredericson, PhD, and Joseph H. Handlon, PhD, "The Later Years from a Gestalt Systems/Field Perspective: Therapeutic Considerations," *Gestalt Review* 7, no. 2 (2003): 95–96.

13. Emmons, *Psychology of Gratitude*, 12.

14. Irvin D. Yalom, *Staring at the Sun: Overcoming the Terror of Death* (San Francisco: Jossey-Bass, 2008), 145.

15. Ibid., 145–46.

16. Belden C. Lane, "Rabbinical Stories: A Primer on Theological Method," *Christian Century* 98:41 (December 16, 1081): 1308–1309.

17. Roberts, *Psychology of Gratitude*, 66–77.

18. Ibid., 69.

19. Bill W., *Alcoholics Anonymous: The Story of How Many Thousands of Men and Women Have Recovered from Alcoholism*, 4th ed. (New York: Alcoholics Anonymous World Services, 2001), 66.

20. Lewis B. Smedes, *Forgive and Forget: Healing the Hurts We Don't Deserve* (San Francisco: HarperSanFrancisco, 1984), 8.

21. Ibid., 20.

22. Ibid., 21.

23. Ibid., 22–23.

24. Ibid., 23.

25. Ibid., 22.

26. Ibid., 29.

27. J. R. Beck "When to Forgive," in *Journal of Psychology and Christianity* 11 (1992): 269–273, quoted by Lise DeShea, "A Scenario-Based Scale of Willingness to Forgive," *Individual Differences Research* 1, no. 3 (2003): 201.

28. Fredericson and Handlon, "The Later Years," 96.

29. Paul Pennick, "Caught in a Trap," *Living Faith*, July 13, 2009.

30. Smedes, 29.

31. Ibid., 27

32. Ibid.

33. Ibid., 27–28.

34. Ibid., 28.

35. Ibid.

36. Terri Mifek, "Away from the Comfort Zone," *Living Faith,* June 22, 2009.

37. Johann Christoph Arnold, *Seventy Times Seven: The Power of Forgiveness* (Farmington, PA: Plough, 1997), 24.

CHAPTER 6

1. Becky Birtha, quoted in Catherine Whitmire, *Plain Living: A Quaker Path to Simplicity* (Notre Dame, IN: Sorin Books, 2001), 67.

2. Pat Schneider, "The Patience of Ordinary Things," *Another River: New and Selected Poems* (Amherst, MA: Amherst Writers & Artists Press, 2005).

3. Nikos Kazantzakis, *Zorba the Greek*, tr. Carl Wildman (New York: Simon and Schuster, 1952), 51.

4. Ludwig Wittgenstein, *Tractus Logico-Philosophicus* (London: Routledge & Kegan Paul, 1961), 44, quoted in Sam Keen, *Apology for Wonder* (New York: Harper and Row, 1969), 22.

5. Abraham J. Heschel, *God in Search of Man: A Philosophy of Judaism* (New York: Harper and Row, 1955), 45.

6. Lloyd Geering, "A Ecological Faith for the Global Era," *Ecotheology* 6.1/6.2 (July 2001): 20.

7. Dag Hammarskjöld, *Markings*, trans. Leif Sjoberg and W. H. Auden (New York: Knopf, 1964), 46.

8. Quoted by James A. Harnish, "Do You Know What Time It Is?" in *Reflections on Aging and Spiritual Growth*, ed. Andrew J. Weaver, Harold G. Koenig, and Phyllis C. Roe (Nashville: Abingdon, 1998), 60.

9. Mary Oliver, "At the River Clarion," *Evidence: Poems by Mary Oliver* (Boston: Beacon, 2009), 53.

10. Joe Robinson, "Blackberries Don't Fit in Bikinis," *Los Angeles Times*, August 13, 2006.

11. Mary Marrocco, *Living Faith*, October 26, 2007.

12. Harold Kushner, *When All You've Ever Wanted Isn't Enough* (New York: Simon and Schuster, 1986), 146–147.

13. Anthony de Mello, *One-Minute Wisdom* (Garden City, NY: Doubleday, 1985), 57.

14. Elizabeth Gilbert, *Eat, Pray, Love: One Woman's Search for Everything across Italy, India and Indonesia* (New York: Viking Penguin, 2006), 132.

15. Phillip Bennett, *Let Yourself Be Loved* (Mahwah, NJ: Paulist Press, 1997), 67–68.

16. Kathleen Fischer, *Winter Grace: Spirituality and Aging* (Nashville, TN: Upper Room Books, 1998), 58–59.

17. Ibid., 60–61.

18. Jared Sandbert, "Counting Blessings? Don't Forget to Tally What Doesn't Irk You," *Wall Street Journal*, November 24, 2004.

19. Fischer, *Winter Grace*, 51.

20. Irvin D. Yalom, *Staring at the Sun: Overcoming the Terror of Death* (San Francisco: Jossey-Bass, 2008), 135–136.

21. Nanoff, *Rising from the Dead*, 5.

22. Marilyn Chandler McEntyre, "Growing in Grace," in *Weavings: A Journal of Christian Spiritual Life* 23:1 (Jan./Feb. 2008), 8.

23. Ibid.

24. We are indebted to Bishop Gordon Bennett, SJ for this insight, shared at a Loyola Marymount University Faculty and Staff Retreat, February 13, 2009.

25. *Los Angeles Times*, May 6, 2007.

26. Philip C. Watkins, "Gratitude and Subjective Well-Being," in *The Psychology of Gratitude*, ed. Robert A. Emmons and Michael E. McCullough (New York: Oxford University Press, 2004), 180.

27. Ibid.

28. Elizabeth Gray Vining, quoted in Catherine Whitmire, *Plain Living: A Quaker Path to Simplicity* (Notre Dame, IN: Sorin Books, 2001), 68.

29. Monica Furlong, "A Spirituality of Aging?" in *Reflections on Aging and Spiritual Growth*, ed. Andrew J. Weaver, Harold G. Koenig, and Phyllis C. Roe, 46.

30. M. Basil Pennington, "Long on the Journey," ibid., 30.

31. Roberta Bondi, ibid., 22.

32. Ibid.

33. Ibid., 23.

34. Ibid., 24.

35. Rabbi Lawrence Kushner, "Introduction to Jewish Spirituality," a three-part video series produced for use with the Professional Developmental Training Program (PDTC) sponsored by the United States Navy Chaplain's Corp for Sea Service Chaplains in 1997.

36. Author unknown.

37. Katherine Whitton, quoted in Whitmire, *Plain Living*, 67–68.

38. Adapted from Stephen Levin, *A Year to Live: How to Live This Year As If It Were Your Last* (New York: Bell Tower), 82–83.

39. Adapted from a reflection proposed by Anthony de Mello, SJ, *Hearts on Fire: Praying with Jesuits* (St. Louis: Institute of Jesuit Sources, 1993), 18–19.

CHAPTER 7

1. Anthony de Mello, *Wellsprings: A Book of Spiritual Exercises* (Garden City, NY: Doubleday, 1986), 239.

2. Karl Rahner, SJ, *The Practice of Faith: A Handbook of Contemporary Spirituality*, ed. Karl Lehmann and Albert Raffelt, trans. John Griffiths (New York: Crossroad, 1983), 22.

3. Marcus Borg, *Jesus: Uncovering the Life, Teachings, and Relevance of a Religious Revolutionary* (New York: HarperCollins, 2006), 131–332.

4. Rahner, *The Practice of Faith*, 22.

5. Karl Rahner, *Belief Today* (New York: Sheed and Ward, 1967), 14.

6. Dennis Hamm, SJ, "Rummaging for God: Praying Backwards through Your Day," in *An Ignatian Spirituality Reader*, ed. George W. Traub, SJ (Chicago: Loyola Press, 2008), 107.

7. Ibid.

8. Belden C. Lane, "Rabbinical Stories: A Primer on Theological Method," *Christian Century* 98:41 (December 16, 1981), 1307.

9. Ignatius of Loyola, *Letters of St. Ignatius of Loyola*, tr. and ed. William J. Young, (Chicago: Loyola University Press, 1959), 55.

10. Henri de Lubac, *Teilhard de Chardin: The Man and His Meaning* (New York: New American Library, 1967), 34.

11. Ibid., 35. Emphasis in the original.

12. Thomas Hart, *Spiritual Quest: A Guide to the Changing Landscape* (Mahwah, NJ: Paulist Press, 1999), 121.

13. Joyce Rupp, OSM, "Rediscovering God in the Midst of Work," in *Handbook of Spirituality for Ministers*, ed. Robert J. Wicks (Mahwah, NJ: Paulist Press, 1995), 262.

14. Ibid.

15. Catherine of Siena, *The Dialogue of the Seraphic Virgin*, quoted by Karen E. Smith, *Christian Spirituality* (London: SCM Press, 2007), 30

16. See Peter Schineller, "St. Ignatius and Creation-Centered Spirituality," *The Way* 29, no. 1 (January 1989): 46–59.

17. Rahner, *The Practice of Faith*, 81.

18. Becky Garrison, "Where is God?" in *Luminos: Faith & Light for the Journey* 122, no. 1 (Spring 2009): 16.

19. Ibid.

20. Eugene H. Peterson, *The Jesus Way: A Conversation on the Ways that Jesus is the Way* (Grand Rapids, MI: Eerdmans, 2007), 55.

21. Howard Gray, SJ, "As I See It," *Company*, Spring 1999.

22. Walter J. Burghardt, "Contemplation: A Long and Loving Look at the Real," *Church* 5, no 4 (Winter, 1989): 14–18.

23. Anthony de Mello, SJ, "The Little Fish," in *The Song of the Bird*, 12–13.

24. Ibid., 13.

25. Fritz Perls quoted in Claudio Naranjo, *The Techniques of Gestalt Therapy* (Berkeley, CA.: SAT Press, 1973), 11.

26. *Spiritual Exercises*, no. 2.

27. *Spiritual Exercises*, no. 11.

28. *Spiritual Exercises*, no. 254.

29. *Spiritual Exercises*, no. 118.

30. Stephen J. Rossetti, "Truly Seeing Jesus and Others," *Living Faith*, July 5, 2009.

31. Peterson, *The Jesus Way*, 45.

32. Elizabeth Barrett Browning, "Aurora Leigh," VII, 821–824.

33. Charles E. O'Neill, SJ, "Acatamiento: Ignatian Reverence in History and in Contemporary Culture," *Studies in the Spirituality of Jesuits* 8, no. 1 (January, 1976): 36.

34. Lawrence Kushner, *Eyes Remade for Wonder: A Lawrence Kushner Reader* (Woodstock, VT: Jewish Lights, 1998), 10.

35. Ibid.

36. Ibid., 10–11.

37. Abraham J. Heschel, *God in Search of Man: A Philosophy of Judaism* (New York: Harper and Row, 1955), 108.

38. Ibid., 106.

39. Ibid., 108.

40. From Robert Wicks, *Touching the Holy* (Notre Dame, IN: Ave Maria Press, 1992), 29, n.15.

41. Nicholas Lash, *Easter in the Ordinary: Reflections on Human Experience and the Knowledge of God* (Notre Dame, IN: University of Notre Dame Press, 1990), 289.

42. Ibid.

43. Ibid., 181.

44. Ibid.

45. This anonymous parable has been circulating orally.

EPILOGUE

1. Patricia Loring, quoted in Catherine Whitmire, *Plain Living: A Quaker Path to Simplicity* (Notre Dame, IN: Sorin Books, 2001), 69.

Index

❧

Important note: **Boldfaced numbers** are the page references for scripture citations, which are indexed alphabetically by name, then numerically by chapter and verse.